THE MIT PRESS

CAMBRIDGE, MASSACHUSETTS — LONDON, ENGLAND

Some Reasons For Traveling To Italy

Peter Wilson

An Italy of his own
Kurt W. Forster

Uncounted travelers have beaten a path to the Italian Peninsula across the centuries. Their recollections have cast a powerful spell over the land, arresting famous sites and monuments in freeze-frame and giving rise to a veritable industry of images. Generations of northern painters and engravers supplied the hotly desired *vedute*, with Piranesi finally inking the monuments so deeply into memory that they assumed an indelible existence of their own. Only photography outdid engravings and drawings in the second half of the nineteenth century, when Italy was among the most thoroughly documented countries—not only for its art and its buildings (indispensable as they were for figures like the Swiss historian Jacob Burckhardt, who acquired a hefty quantity of images in the new medium), but also for its landscape and folklore. The desire for an Italy that would reveal its true nature and take its place in collective memory sought its fulfillment in travel and in the global circulation of artifacts and souvenirs. Such is the dilemma of Italy to this day: love it or leave it; buy it or steal it: whatever the case may be, few can do without it.

Contemporary tourism could not have evolved the way it did without Italy being crisscrossed and its map endlessly crosshatched by generations of travelers. The guidebook became a category of literature in its own right. During the sixteenth century, more and more erudite commentaries instructed foreigners on the secrets and peculiarities of a people who, during their long history, were as often losers as conquerors. Unvanquished only in the arts, the various regions were notorious for inspiring groundless enthusiasm or causing bitter disappointment, often in alternation, or even in a confusing mixture of the two. The inhabitants remained largely incomprehensible to foreigners, but this hardly detracted from

Anton Goubau, *The Study of Art in Rome*, 1662
Koninklijk Museum voor Schone Kunsten, Antwerp
© Lukas / Art in Flanders VZW

their charm. The longer visitors stayed around and the deeper they involved themselves in Italian life, the more Italians grew aware that they were characters in a play scripted by others, and that they, as the cast, enacted dramas whose true form was to be the libretti of opera, and later, of film.

In turn, Italians began emigrating in large numbers, bringing to their new homes an earthy or artistic attitude, whether they were architects or bricklayers, singers or symphony players, chefs or waiters, barbers or fashion designers. While their peregrinations left a lasting mark in other countries, a reverse migration by writers like Stendhal (who was besotted by Italy and its music) consolidated the country's reputation as a sphinx of *la dolce vita* and a preserve of archaic ways. In modern times, foreigners who have taken up permanent residence in Italy include scholars such as Bernard Berenson, the Pomeranian Darwinist Anton Dohrn (founder of the *Stazione Zoologica* in Naples) and, in more recent decades, the German composer Hans Werner Henze, the Austrian writer Ingeborg Bachmann and the American painter Cy Twombly. In one form or another, a Rome Prize figures among the most coveted distinctions an artist can obtain. Governments and universities of many other countries have established cultural institutions in Italy, and their role in evaluating, documenting, and in some instances saving works of art and architecture is probably unparalleled in Europe.

While abounding in character, intrigue and even exotic appeal, Italy for many centuries lacked a national identity. It was formed as a composite of many small city-states and communes, some of grand ambition and proud standing, others repeatedly annexed by neighboring powers, but all ultimately subsumed into a grand theater where an infinite variety of cultural remains coalesced to form an unforgettable scenery. Italy offered itself up as a stage on which foreigners could project their own desires, passions and ideas, gradually transforming the entire country into a theatrical setting for the enactment of their own lives.

After the Second World War, no other European country shed the guise of an enemy as swiftly as Italy. A 1941 photography exhibition put on by the Warburg Institute, titled *English Art and the Mediterranean*, had kept alive the memory (if not the prospect) of Italy—its archaeology, and its significance in post-antique art—and the country quickly restored its attractiveness as a holiday destination and nostalgic haven of the avant-garde. Having made jubilant forays during the interwar period with a sunbathed modernism—a far cry from the Nibelungen architecture of Germany—Italian design soon swept western Europe on the heels of Italian cooking and fashion. At the same time, Milanese architecture studios such as BBPR and Gio Ponti, young architects like Aldo Rossi, and historians like Bruno Zevi and Manfredo Tafuri were gaining an international audience. Accompanied by espresso, the films of Antonioni, Visconti and Fellini made a grand *entrée* into the Anglo-Saxon world of the 1960s and 1970s, conveniently followed by chairs, lamps, typewriters, and wireless sets of a distinctive design that conjured memories with a whiff of things to come.

Peter Wilson lists all the reasons—more, in fact, than one can credibly come up with—for which Italy retains its hold on our imaginations and continues to stir our senses. In rediscovering the things that have delighted others he refreshes them with an unvarnished take of his own. It was a stroke of genius on his part to use the mobile phone—the *telefonino*, as it is affectionately called in Italy, a verbal caress of its diminutive size and intimate use—as the means of transport for the imagination, as the Pegasus who carries him swiftly from one place to the next, keeping him aloft and his spirit alert. But just as his experience of Italy becomes the stuff of his imagination, it is also brought back to the source, taking the form of projects that offer all he has learned to a sometimes reluctant host. The Bolles+Wilson design for the European Library in Milan—still languishing in the labyrinthine underground of Italian bureaucracy— could singularly redeem that city's provincial self-absorption with a building of truly European character, the likes of which no Italian architect could conceivably conjure at this time. Their urban interventions in Monteluce in Perugia, on the other hand, raise latent conditions to a level of presence that is heightened by a sense of urban interiority that one might have expected to emerge from nowhere other than Italy. Except it didn't, and the city had to await a foreigner's interaction with circumstances that have assumed a stale familiarity for locals. It is a classic case of those best acquainted with a situation being least able to understand it, of closeness obscuring the view, and familiarity erecting barriers. What Bolles+Wilson have been able to do with their Italian projects is to awaken local somnambulists and surprise them with something they might have been the first to come up with, if only they had been able to take a critical step back from their everyday life.

In a similar vein, Peter Wilson's drawings and watercolors coax Italian landscapes out of the image preserves in which painters of the last centuries have embedded them. A most interesting transformation begins to stir inside his images—as if he has dialed into the past, not to rouse long-departed spirits, but to trigger new life in his perceptions of the country in its present state. In doing so he has hit upon a form of telecommunication, if not telepathy—a way of measuring images with his response to a past that would not exist were it not for our present interest in it, especially our curiosity about its latent possibilities, its dormant beauties, and an infinitely intriguing future that might still spring from it.

Rome from the Baths of Caracalla, after Jacob Philipp Hackert, 2012
$5\frac{3}{32} \times 5\frac{3}{32}$" (13 × 13 CM)

Viaggio in Italia

Toni was the first Italian I ever met, when I was only four years old. He would appear every weekend, riding a mammoth and thunderous Moto Guzzi complete with sidecar. In actual fact there must have been at least three Tonis employed to assist my father in paving, building fences, and generally constructing the world of my childhood. It was Toni who forgot to close the white wooden orchard gate through which my pony wandered to test the hessian ground that in winter covered the newly completed swimming pool. By the time the new cream-colored pony named Panna arrived, I was a teenager, and it must have been another Toni (Toni Three?) who left the gate open for her to escape and fill the pool with a potent liquid fertilizer which, over the next few months, did wonders for our ever-expanding garden.

As postwar Italian immigrants the Tonis could barely, to our Strine-tuned ears, "speaka da English." For hats they wore brown paper bags with the sides folded up—protection from the Sicilian-strength Australian sun. My father was fond of them. They reminded him of his Italian wartime experience with the 7th Armored Brigade, which I imagine as something like Roberto Rossellini's neorealist masterpiece *Paisà*. My father was not one of the GIs losing his innocence fighting northward, but more the British Major sitting, calmly disengaged, in the Boboli Gardens overlooking a contested Florence, identifying church towers and other cultural landmarks through his binoculars as Italian partisans holding rooftops and building interiors skirmished with the retreating Germans who held the streets—a topological striation of strife. He never spoke of his Italian war except to give one gruesome recollection: as an engineer, his job was to get the tanks rolling. If they were hit, his men would have to scrape away bits of crew from the interiors. His nickname for me was Piccolo Pietro.

In 1955 the Wilson family sailed on the PNO *Orion*, across the Indian Ocean, through the Suez Canal, and on June 13 docked in Napoli. Business trips from Australia to Europe at that time took six months. My Italy-seasoned father took over the diary notes for this day:

Venice, 2013
$3 \times 2^{13}\!/\!_{16}$" (7.5 × 7 CM)

"Disembarked at approx 1pm. Hired a car (Cadillac Cabriolet) for the remainder of the day ... left the dock area ... bombed during the war ... one-room sheds built from rubble ... people living in appalling conditions ... the Autostrada, most direct way to Pompeii ... visited the ruins for half an hour. Vesuvius appears to be extinct ... drink at bar costs 12 shillings for two beers, two cokes, and one lemonade. Proceed via Vietri sul Mare ... congested living and cultivation ... produce carried on donkeys in standard-size baskets ... a blindfolded horse working a water pump ... the same road I traversed during the war with the 7th Army Division ... took the coast road through Ravello, Amalfi, Positano, and Sorrento ... clings to the mountainside, hairpin bends, tunnels, houses perched in the most inaccessible positions ... remarkable they do not slide into the sea ... every square foot used for growing ... lemons horizontally and underneath sweet corn. A kilometer before Amal halted as a procession rounded the next bend ... first small children, then priests with nondescript crosses ... then four men with a shoulder-high St Anthony effigy (patron of lost things) ... then a brass band and a collection of all

sorts of people (some lost) ... better to be stopped as the road is not wide enough to pass. A little way past Amal we hear a loud report ... driver stops, looks under the car ... comes up with a smile ... "bombe esta!" (reworks). Arrived Sorrento at 8pm ... not 6pm as promised ... dinner at the Terrelino Hotel, lights and the view across the bay to Naples impressive, also the sheer drop from the hotel balcony ... children tired but the Italian waiters made an impression ... the meal was quite a change from ship food and a bottle of Ru no Chianti excellent ... For four and three children it cost 9,000 lire (£5). Arrived back at the ship at 10.45pm having covered over 100 miles for £15 pounds plus £2 tip.

After Hubert Robert, *A Young Frenchman Engaging with a Corinthian Capital*, 2013
$1^{19}\!/_{32} \times 2^{5}\!/_{16}$" (4 × 6 CM)

Films serve to augment and give structure to the punctured templates of memory. Some 20 years later I recognized one of the Tonis as the maniacal motorbike rider who roared through almost every scene of Fellini's 1973 *Amarcord*. Rossellini's 1954 *Viaggio in Italia*, with Ingrid Bergman and George Sanders as a British couple under a tension magnified by their context, also brings to mind my parents' sojourn in Venice one year after the film was released. This time my mother's culturally inexperienced gaze indexes the diary notes with a glaze of sober pragmatism:

Thursday September 29—left Innsbruck 9.30am ... across the Brenner ... glorious scenery ... into Italy, through the Dolomites, again glorious scenery ... took a picture of a ski-jump ... appeared to be very important ... reached Venice 5.30pm. Motorboat to Danieli, settled, dressed for dinner—cost £6. Strolled ... lots of buildings are showing signs of crumbling, our hotel walls are not square by any means ... listened to hotel orchestra for 1/2 hour before retiring. Friday 30th, hired a gondola ... Grand Canal, Rialto Bridge ... glass blowing ... feeling a bit weary, back to Danieli 5pm ... 7pm caught ferry to Lido, freezing cold, everything closed ... one look at the Casino and launch back to Venice ... bought cards for the children. Sat October 1st ... up bright and early, launch to garage ... left Venice 9.30am ... rather glad to be on our way, don't think we will be going there again ... motored across to Bergamo ... lunch by lake in Como ... pretty ... and across the Swiss border at Chiasso ... not a very good impression of Italians.

Ravello Breakfast, 2010
1 $^{19}\!/_{32}$ × 3" (4 × 7.5 CM)

In the 1970s I arrived back in Europe as a 20-something from Australia. The expected itinerary was to follow the "grand template" of the Grand Tour. With the wide Australian horizon as my yardstick, I imagined the grandeur of the continent being like a pocket handkerchief—easily folded to size. In Amsterdam we purchased a moped and rode to Copenhagen, then turned back and headed south to Italy. This mode of travel was not particularly reminiscent of the nineteenth-century grand tourists, carried by sedan chairs, but was comparable to their Alpine crossings in terms of both terror and the Enlightenment aesthetic register of Edmund Burke's sublimity—one day walking the moped uphill, and the next day rolling down.

After Giovanni Battista Lusieri, *The Temple of Serapis*
(With Phantom Tourists), 2013
$2^{3}/_{16} \times 3"$ (5.5 × 7.5 CM)

It is not expected that the Italy described in these pages will correspond to the Italy of the general consensus, the Italy as lived by Italians, or the Italy visited by countless tourists intent on gazing beyond the quotidian details of their non-Italian lives. Much of what follows is the product of cartographic imagination. Place names perform the function of magical talismans, and the mind instills them with color and detail. Such narratives—illusory spaces—do not necessarily tally with received or sanitized history, or with the exact topographies of real places. Seen in this way, *Some Reasons* represents a painting into the scene—historical reworkings, appropriations, and a scrutiny of specific Italian tropes and topographies with the eye of an architect—often with the intention to rescript them.

The Bolles+Wilson design for the new quarter of Monteluce in Perugia is the most actual and consequential of such revisions, but more recently still, in a time of pandemic, the actual has been superseded by the virtual, or at least by Google Streetview and Zoom brainstorming sessions. This was the procedure for a 2020 competition for the Bagnoli Zone just north of Naples, a heavily polluted brownfield site which was to be rescripted as a new urban park. In our scheme, circular cutouts in the thick carpet of Mediterranean pine frame reuses of industrial archaeology, while brave visitors fly—from zip tower to zip tower—over a beach, marina, and science center. The whole composition is overseen by the one-eyed face of an adjacent Cyclops Hotel, located on an outcrop called Cyclops Island.

Bolles+Wilson, Monteluce masterplan, Perugia, 2006
$4^{11}/_{16} \times 9^{13}/_{16}$" (12 × 25 CM)

But this same cyclops and Cyclops Island in some sense also oversees this book, if only because this island was supposedly visited by Ulysses, the first person to travel to Italy. Under this same watchful eye, thirty-five years after my moped first crossed over the border, my own reasons for traveling to Italy have gone beyond the easy list—holiday, food, culture, with the Grand Tour as the most obvious of tropes. These motives only scratched the surface of deeply rooted personal experience, architectural habit, and a wider cultural mythology. From my explorations of Milan, Venice, Perugia, and Naples, Italian cities have been points of reference for much of my professional life, with their grains and details revealing immeasurable reasons for turning around and heading south.

Bolles+Wilson, with Ottovini Associates, Urban Park, Naples,
with Cyclops Hotel on the actual Cyclops Island, 2020
$4^{11}/_{16} \times 9^{13}/_{16}$" (12 × 25 CM)

Some Reasons For Traveling To Italy

To dream Italy

Freud's Wall, Berggasse 19, Vienna, 2013
2 × 2" (5 × 5 CM)

For Freud photographs were a form of involuntary memory that invaded phantasms and dreams. Goethe in 1789 had written that all the dreams of his youth came to life when he finally came to Rome. In Freud's case he actually dreamt Rome before traveling to Italy. "I dreamt once that I was looking out of a railway carriage window at the Tiber and the Ponte Sant' Angelo ... the view that I had seen in my dream was taken from a well-known engraving which I had caught sight of the day before..."

The view was a popular postcard subject, the sort often sent from Rome to Vienna, and Freud's dream image framed by a window was essentially photographic, a then relatively new medium that communicated directly without filters of representational decoding.

Memory for Freud was like the slide show he himself experienced in 1907, a lantern projection on a canvas screen hung from a rooftop in Rome's Piazza Colonna. Among the advertisements (*fotoreclami*) were interspersed fantastical subjects—landscapes, ethnographic scenes (Congo), glacial ascents—mnemic images—an indiscriminate

Matisse Mimes Freud, 2015

$5\frac{3}{32} \times 6\frac{5}{16}$" (13 × 16 CM)

mix like the juxtaposed images in a postcard collection that induce a detached way of seeing not dissimilar to the Freudian phenomenon of spectatorship in dream. The Piazza Colonna experience (public viewing) could thus be understood as a sort of shared dream-state.

Michelangelo's Moses for the tomb of Pope Julius II played a significant role in Freud's personal biography. His 1914 analysis cast its monumental stasis as concluding an emotional narrative, for Freud the Moses statue was perhaps even a vehicle of reconciliation between his own Jewishness and western culture. He wrote to his friend Ernst Förster, then traveling to Rome, to "bring my deepest devotion to Moses and write me about him." Freud also wrote to Wilhelm Fleiss in 1897 that "my longing for Rome is, by the way, deeply neurotic." Papal Rome has been interpreted as the "father" image to be feared and the eternal *Urbs* as "mother" with all the Oedipian reverberations of Goethe's ROMA-AMOR equation.

In 1876 a young, unmarried Freud wrote from Trieste (still part of the Austrian Empire), "the cats are beautiful and friendly, but the women especially distinctive."

On his first trip to Rome in 1901 Freud took special interest in the Laocoön statue in the Vatican Belvedere, a subject illustrated in photographic books by Furtwängler, Löwy and Duchenne in his library. Freud's interpretation followed Lessing's in reading Laocoön as suppressing rather than expressing a cry of pain— *Selbstüberwindung*—a self-control or dominance over the superego, a reading that also activates Warburg's concept of *Pathosformel*, an intertwining of feelings and movement.

Freud climbed Vesuvius in 1902 with his brother Alexander, visiting the National Archaeological Museum in Naples as well as Pompeii, that most physical metaphor for forgetfulness and retrieval.

"There is, in fact, no better analogy for repression…(than Pompeii)," wrote Freud in *Delusions and Dreams*. In *Gravida: A Pompeiian Fantasy*, a 1907 novella by the writer and poet Wilhelm Jensen, an archaeologist (Hanold) observes a plaster cast of a beautiful girl come to life. This Pompeiian hallucination triggered Freud's exploration of the archaeological metaphor for psychoanalysis; the theme was Lithophilia (Pygmalionism), fetishized erotic love of statues resulting from suppressed desire.

In 1910 Freud wrote from Syracuse of the melancholic torpor that clouded his mind while visiting the Temple of Apollo. "Uncanny" (*unheimlich*) was how he described the paralyzing atmosphere of oppressive silence. A hot wind from Africa (*scirocco*) had long been *associated* with melancholy, and a clouded intelligence that supposedly heightened a Romantic receptivity to art and nature.

Hackert's telefonino

Characters
JAKOB PHILIPP HACKERT
CHARLES GORE
RICHARD PAYNE KNIGHT

CHARLES GORE I say Hackert, might that be your telefonino?

JAKOB PHILIPP HACKERT Ja, Gore, but be a good fellow und use it to call Goethe, who will soon be arriving in Rome. We must inform him zat we are here on the 27th of May 1777, beside the ruined tower of Empedocles.

CG Hang on a minute, old chap. I do think Knight should use it first to inform Mr Burke of this sublime Etna eruption. What was that you just said, Knight? The wind stole your words.

RICHARD PAYNE KNIGHT They were addressed neither to you, Gore, nor to Herr Hackert, nor to his frozen dog Peliccione. I was simply remarking, for posterity, that "I felt myself elevated above humanity & looked down with contempt upon the mighty objects of ambition under me."

CG If Hackert's telefonino is the object to which you refer, might I make the observation that its presence in this setup is as questionable as our own?

RPK Ha, Gore, and who is responsible for sowing the seeds of doubt? Not poor Hackert, who is so busy pumping out *vedute* for us English dilettanti that it will take him six more years to commit the three of us here on Etna to gouache (244 × 358mm), whereas his pupil chum, Balthasar Anton Dunker, whipped out a lithograph to flog to all and sundry that same year. A runner I might add. I myself will most likely bequeath my Dunker (and even a few of your amateur scratchings, which Hackert takes such pains to correct) to the British Museum.

CG Hang on old chap, don't forget that fleabag hiding behind the label "Anonimo Napoletano," whose scurrilous *incisione* is directly pilfered from Hackert and Dunker but—to my great personal injury—depicts only two surviving figures. Myself and the mutt Peliccione are edited, gone, erased from history.

RPK Now you're getting warm, Gorey. One could well enquire which media might be responsible for evaporating your good self? Who was it that subsequently copied that froggo Houel's figures into his less than original drawing (262 × 343mm, Klassik Stiftung Weimar, Graphische Sammlungen) of that desperate Goat's Grotto we were forced to put up in last night? You had the nerve to ascribe the names of Richard Payne Knight, Jakob Philipp Hackert, and Charles Gore to the appropriated scruffy figures, and then to top it all, the erroneous detail which diligent art historians (Andreas Stolzenburg) could not fail to spot: that tree in full bloom, casting my diary notes of snowflakes and the first buds of spring into historiographic disrepute. You even managed to transform poor Peliccione into a night-black mongrel.

Hackert's Telefonino I, after Jakob Philipp Hackert,
The Crater of Etna with the Ruined Tower of Empedocles, 2011
$8\,^{11}\!/_{16} \times 5\,^{1}\!/_{2}$" (22 × 14 CM)

CG You're one to talk, Knight! You'll probably trot back to the realm of King George and pursue an illustrious career theorizing the picturesque. I'll have you know that Jean-Pierre-Louis-Laurent Houel, whose details I did indeed have cause to quote, includes in his four-volume *Voyage pittoresque des Isles de Sicile, de Malte et de Lipari* (1782–87) the exact scene in which we now stand. Picturesque—ha! Etna is not erupting at all, the supposed Tower of Empedocles is being hastily thrown together by a pair of rustics, a mimetic prop for us grand tourists no doubt, and we three gentlemen, you with cane and wide cap, me in my elegant blue cape (here I thank Herr Hackert for the accuracy of his memory) are rendered as lumpy ruffians, rude staffs in hand, more concerned with holding onto their hats than with the sublime panorama unfolding before them.

JPH Gentlemen, gentlemen, allow me, the artist responsible for this contrivance, to remind you zat you are both British. It may vell be zat those colonists are right now giving you a spot of trouble on ze other side of the Atlantic but all ze more reason to take a long-term perspective on image status, forms of visibility, originality, technology, reproducibility. All art is construct, even more so when it brings me a healthy income. It may well be zat I have grafted one of Hamilton's Vesuvius eruptions onto the Sicilian peak, and yes indeed, zat is my telefonino. I urge you to take it as a memento mori, a fold in time—a counterfactual history, if I may so anticipate Signor Borges.

JPH Well said, Hackert, old chap, it is a pleasure indeed to take instruction from you.

CG A sentiment we would also have no hesitation extending to your esteemed countrymen Goethe and Winckelmann.

The new industrial wealth of his grandfather, a Shropshire iron-foundry owner, enabled Richard Payne Knight to pursue a career as both author and connoisseur. He was a sickly child and educated at home. However in 1772 after receiving his inheritance Payne Knight had commissioned his new home, Downton Castle, and set off on his first Italian tour. Four years later he made a second trip—initially to Rome with the watercolorist John Robert Cozens before traveling to Sicily in the spring of 1777, accompanied by Jakob Philipp Hackert and Charles Gore. During their two-month journey he prepared the elaborate travelogue *Expedition into Sicily*, which details, almost archaeologically, the ruins of Segesta, Selinunte, and Agrigento. His traveling companions supplied the book's images—lush watercolors of landscapes that often depict the three windswept travelers convening at the base of an excavation or taking in a view. After the trip, Knight asked Cozens to rework certain drawings, and Thomas Hearne was later commissioned to produce a number of watercolors for engraving. Knight returned to England in 1777 and by his thirtieth birthday had completed the building of Downton Castle in Shropshire (replete with a domed dining room based on the Pantheon), entered Parliament, joined the Society of Dilettanti and vehemently opposed the British Museum's purchase of the Elgin Marbles, on the grounds that they were "second-rate." Never married, Knight was drawn to antique representations of the male generative organ, an interest also shared by the Danish sculptor Bertel Thorvaldsen and by Goethe, who worked the Graeco-Roman phallic god into his *Roman Elegies* of 1788–90. Knight's 1786 *Discourse on the Worship of Priapus*, which argued for the persistence of pagan practices in modern culture, inevitably led to his condemnation as a libertine. In prioritizing eroticism over Judaeo-Christian puritanism—in essence a scholarly libertinism—he stood for a radical moral disengagement from the socio-symbolic norms of his time, a stance that cast Payne Knight as a predecessor to neo-paganism and the cabalist-occult philosophy of Aleister Crowley. A contemporary reading would perhaps better locate such transgression within the rubric of Lacan's fourth agency, the law of desire.

Richard Payne Knight,
after Thomas Lawrence, 2012
3³⁄₃₂ × 2" (8 × 5 CM)

Knight's interests veered into other earthly delights. The fashionably sublime Etna eruption gave him a greater appreciation of "wilder and even more natural gardens," as opposed to the "romantic landscape." His 1794 "The Landscape, a didactic poem" instructively pointed out the inherent deficiencies of Capability Brown's "smooth and monotonous gardens:" "Nymphs and dryads can find no sanctuary among Brown's bare and tidy scenes." His own garden, Downton Vale, was described in painterly idioms as a place "where sympathy with terror is combined, to move, to melt, and elevate the mind." According to Payne Knight, Brown's turf did not live up to that of Claude or Poussin, nor to the dense iconographic and emblematic codings at Stowe or Stourhead. Mid-century garden taste, he argued, offered Edmund Burke's beauty but not his sublime. What Knight was ultimately chronicling and championing was a paradigm shift from an informed iconographic decoding to a subjective empowerment of the senses. A decade later, in his 1804 *Analytical Inquiry into the Principles of Taste* (a work much indebted to Burke), he defined the picturesque not as an objective characteristic of the landscape, but as something located in the mind of the observer, which could only be activated by an informed association of picture and landscape, landscape and picture; a subjective perception where qualities melt into one another and intellect complements sense and imagination.

CHARLES GORE (1729–1807)

Charles Gore belonged to what William Makepeace Thackeray in *Vanity Fair* termed "a good company of English fugitives." His 1751 marriage to the rope-making and shipbuilding heiress Mary Cockerell made him independently wealthy, enabling him to pursue his hobbies as an amateur yachtsman and draftsman: he designed his own cutter (*The Snail*), cruised the English coast in the company of the royal dukes, honed his drawing abilities, producing numerous pictorial records of his maritime excursions—he even went so far as to copy or amend a number of works by Willem van de Velde, among them *The Dutch Fleet* (1774), now hanging in the National Maritime Museum in Greenwich. In 1773, Mary's ill health took the Gore family south, from Southampton to Lisbon. From there they eventually made their way to Italy on the frigate *Levant*. Not long after their arrival in Florence the Gores sat for a family portrait painted by Johann Zoffany to commemorate the engagement of Charles' eldest daughter Hannah Anne, then 15, to the much older "Italian" Earl Cowper.

In Rome, possibly through a shared interest in nautical subjects, amateur painter Gore met professional painter Hackert and became a regular at the latter's studio at 9 Piazza di Spagna, where the other Gore daughters, Emily and Eliza, took painting lessons (according to Goethe, Hackert claimed Eliza Gore was his most gifted pupil).

In April 1777, Hackert and Gore set off with Richard Payne Knight on a six-week expedition to Paestum, Syracuse, and Etna. On this trip, Gore drew with the aid of a camera obscura, often corrected in Hackert's hand (the English nobleman in Goethe's *Elective Affinities*, for whom Gore was the inspiration, "was occupied most of the day by taking picturesque views of the park with the help of a dark box"). He also produced 40 drawings for Knight's *Expedition into Sicily* and 154 watercolors of his own, today found in the Weimar Graphic Archive. In 1779, after four years in Italy, Gore and family returned to London, where both he and Knight were elected to the Society of Dilettanti.

In 1791, following the death of his wife, Charles and his daughters relocated to Weimar, settling at Goethe's former residence, the Jaegerhaus. The move was encouraged by the Grand Duke, Karl August, who had his beady eye on "die schöne Emilie." Goethe himself was just starting to write the account of his three-year *Italian Journey*, for which he used the sketches of Hackert and Gore as an *aide-mémoire*. But despite their firm standing as court favorites, Charles Gore and his daughters were not at the center of Goethe's social orbit.

"The Gores are great provided you can fit in with their ways, but they are so moralistic in their outlook and so limited in their knowledge of art that I scarcely know what to say to them," he told a mutual friend, Charlotte von Stein. "They are happy in themselves, and I don't want to interfere with their happiness, given how little I can partake of it."

While the Grand Tour provided the ideal stage for the intermingling of new and inherited privilege, Gore himself rejected the conventions and social props of a rapidly transforming English society for the stable (if parochial) feudal rituals of the Weimar court—evidence of a trajectory somewhat counter-cyclical to the grand narratives of democratic and social evolution then unfolding.

His own self-doubt, his less than masterful artistic abilities (his daughters were said to have more talent), and perhaps a certain level of social insecurity about the radical eighteenth-century paradigm shifts of English class hierarchies resulted in an attachment anxiety. An over-identification with his role models, Hackert and Goethe, shows Gore defining himself through a symbiotic absorption of foreign influences—a mimetic association with a stronger "other" that would lead to the copying and signing of works and, not surprisingly, future problems for art historians.

JAKOB PHILIPP HACKERT (1737–1807)

After graduating from the academy in Berlin and sojourning in both Stralsund and Paris, Jakob Philipp Hackert had established enough contacts to secure his new enterprise in Italy. He arrived in Rome in 1768—the same year that Laurence Sterne published *Sentimental Journey* and Captain Cook voyaged to the South Seas—with the aim of becoming an efficient market-oriented Mediterranean and Arcadian landscape painter. He spent the next 18 years finding and inventing scenic vistas for his growing client base, alternating his commissions for the *ancien régime* courts of Germany, Russia, Poland, and Naples with those made for his principal client strata— English travelers versed in the classics, fluent in the new taste of landscape decoding, and thus easily ensnared by the Stowe template that often underpinned his compositions: a round antique temple on the left, a bucolic dividing Styx stream, worthy figures under a tree to the right. These were young men of the Grand Tour confronting the "otherness" of Italy, sharing in the aesthetic experience of Empire bonding—implicit snobs confirming their own moral superiority over the modern Romans, whom they cast as the personification of the universal decay of human nature.

Hackert's strict and ordered style was matched by a business-like Prussian efficiency in production and marketing. One brother, Johann Gottlieb Hackert (1744–1773), delivered and drummed up new clients in England while another, Georg (1755–1805), assisted Hackert locally, printing lithographic reproductions (the industrious serialization and distribution of a Mediterranean parallel world).

Hackert's Telefonino II, after Jakob Philipp Hackert,
The English Garden at Caserta, 2011
$1\,^{31}/_{32} \times 9\,^{27}/_{32}$" (5 × 25 CM)

In Rome, Hackert fell in with Angelika Kauffmann's salon, which included Johann Friedrich Reiffenstein (1719–1793), successor to Winckelmann (murdered in 1768 in Trieste by a ruffian pick up) as the principal antiquarian of Rome. After receiving several commissions from King Ferdinand IV of Naples, Hackert relocated in 1786 to take up the secure station of court painter, producing Pompeii excavations (1787) and an idealized bustling and colorful Neapolitan port series—less than accurate representations of the miserable, impoverished and stilted reality, and an illusion the King happily accepted, as the responsibility of civic improvement was an unwanted distraction from his passion for hunting (also documented in exact detail by Hackert).

The success of Hackert's neoclassical style was due in part to a topographic and iconographic double-coding. A scientific Enlightenment gaze of hyper-realistic detail, meticulously recording the zoological, geological, and botanical enfolded in fictive topographies—idealized Arcadian landscapes peopled by rustics or allegorical ancients (such double-coding is reiterated today in digital rendering, where precise photographic fragments seamlessly morph together to give the bling of plausibility to virtual objects and environments).

When French troops entered Naples in 1799, Nelson whisked away the Bourbon king to the relative safety of Sicily (with the Hamiltons also on board), while Hackert (with Tischbein) fled to Pisa and Florence. Once Europe's most renowned landscape painter, Hackert fell into almost total eclipse in the nineteenth century, despite Goethe's championing of his strict neoclassical style against the subjectivity of the new Romantic paradigm. Hackert's trajectory highlights a paradigmatic change that characterizes the closing years of the eighteenth century, a shift from the "experience of Nature" to the "nature of Experience" (Knight's theme: the sublime). A number of Hackerts were among Albert Speer's secret South American art stash, auctioned off anonymously after his release from Spandau.

Etna, 1789 Eruption, 2015
5 5/16 × 5 5/16" (13.5 × 13.5 CM)

Sir William Hamilton, diplomat, antiquarian, equerry to George III, geologist and amateur volcanologist, climbed Vesuvius 22 times during his first four years in Naples. "It is with great difficulty you ascend," he wrote to his daughter Polly. "I had five men to get me up; two before, whose girdles I laid hold of; and three behind, who pushed me by the back. I approached right to the opening ... but could see very little." Despite selling his first collection of vases (the inspiration for Josiah Wedgwood's Etruscan collection) to the British Museum for a reported £8,400, Hamilton soon ran into debt, his daily stipend of £5 as "envoy-extraordinary" in Naples not being commensurate to his passion for accumulating art.

Wedgwood's Etruscan Collection, 2022
$3^{15}/_{16} \times 5^{1}/_{2}$" (10 × 14 CM)

With his marriage to his second wife, Emma (the mistress of Lord Nelson), Hamilton's collecting habit took on a life of its own. Encouraged by her spouse, Emma would dress in Greek costumes to entertain their guests. One of them, a Sir Morritt, described how "with the assistance of one or two Etruscan vases and an urn" Emma became "a Sibyl, then a Fury, a Niobe, a Sophonisba drinking poison, a Bacchante drinking wine, dancing and playing the tambourine, an Agrippina at the tomb of Germanicus and every attitude of almost every different passion." Horace Walpole quipped, "Sir William Hamilton has actually married his gallery of statues."

Hamilton, who spent a total of 35 years in Italy, found many ways to transmit his obsessions back to the British public. He sent detailed specimens and observations of Vesuvius to the Royal Society in London, which disseminated his findings throughout various scientific journals. At the same time, a systematic and extensive importation of paintings and antiquities (both actual and simulated, for the compulsive collector was often duped) helped to legitimize British imperial and colonial ambitions. The industrial-scale importing of mementos appropriated the symbolism and associative tropes of Imperial Rome (a concurrently unfolding counter-reformation baroque was of little interest to the English, who a few years earlier had imported the Hanoverian Georges to exorcise themselves of the papist Stuarts). While Hackert, like Claude and Poussin, produced such transportable imagery, the Hamilton-types of Italy ensured there was an English market to transport it home—a cultural programming through the dissemination of an Arcadia peppered with Augustinian props, a validation of not only Empire but also the picturesque.

IL GIARDINO INGLESE — DER ENGLISCHE GARTEN

Throughout the 1780s Hackert closely observed Hamilton and John Graefer's construction of a 50-acre English garden at the Palazzo Reale in Caserta. Theirs was a mnemonic reconstruction of Arcadia that both returned to and overlaid its locus of origin. Hackert painted the garden in 1793 as gouache, then in 1797 as oil. Both depict a rolling turf filled with botanical details (myrtle), grazing sheep, and picnicking ladies (accompanied by the dog, Peliccione), and purging

Hotel Empedocles, collage after Jakob Philipp Hackert, 2011

$7\frac{5}{16} \times 5\frac{1}{2}$" (18.5 × 14 CM)

all emblematic props in accordance with late eighteenth-century taste. In the background, the "delightful horror" of a smoking Vesuvius makes reference to Burke's sublime. In a letter to Graf Dönhoff von Dönhoffstädt, a friend and client, Hackert described his paintings of English gardens in the foreground with the Italian *veduta* behind them as a "new genre."

In his 1770 essay "On Modern Gardening," Horace Walpole wrote "enough has been done to establish such a school of landscape [gardening].... If we have the seeds of a Claude ... he must come forth." Following the death of the landscape painter Richard Wilson in 1782, it was Hackert who took up this role, dispatching from Italy the painted allegorical and topographic reification of what was then the well-established genre of the English landscape garden—a necessary component in activating and informing the mirrored discursive field of the picturesque.

ERUPTIONS

The lure of an active volcano kept grand tourists coming to Naples throughout the 1700s. Artists had been capturing a smoking Vesuvius for more than a century—from Athanasius Kircher's section view into the volcano (1664) to Hackert's flaming night scene of a 1774 eruption. For London audiences, aroused with curiosity but unable to make the journey to Italy, the collector and amateur volcanologist William Hamilton invented the *Vesuvian Apparatus*, a volcano-machine that used moving pictures, sound and lighting to simulate eruption effects. Other volcanoes proved irresistible: Hackert, Gore, and Payne Knight climbed Mount Etna on May 27, 1777. On returning to Rome from Sicily, Knight commissioned Cozens to work up Gore's sketch of the active volcano. It erupted almost exactly four months after their expedition, on September 29. In addition to his depiction of Vesuvius, Hackert also completed two versions of Etna—one smoking, one erupting, in 1783 and 1790. 1783 was the same year the Icelandic volcano Lakagígar erupted, spewing out an estimated 14km³ of lava over a period of eight months. A red fog of ash and sulphur dioxide engulfed the northern hemisphere, blocking the sun and instigating a drastic three-year climate change that resulted in the coldest recorded winter — the North Sea froze, and in New Orleans the Mississippi River froze. There were droughts in India, and the rice crop failed in Japan. An estimated six million people died from the resulting famine. After three such winters Goethe quit Weimar for Italy. On arriving in Naples he noted the Neapolitan opinion of northern Europe: "*sempre neve, case di legno, gran ignoranza, ma denari assai*" (always snow, wooden houses, huge ignorance, but money enough).

PELICCIONE

Hackert's much-traveled (English Gardens, Pompeii, Etna, Antiquity) dog appears more than 50 times in his master's works.

TELEFONINO

A highly addictive communication device used by the ex-Italian Prime Minister Silvio Berlusconi (secretly recorded by *Independent* editor Valter Lavitola) to allegedly express his inability to imagine sexual intercourse with Angela Merkel, his German counterpart.

EMPEDOCLES 490–430 BC

The pre-Socratic philosopher and citizen of the Greek colony of Agrigentum (in Sicily) is credited as the originator of the cosmogenic theory of the four classical elements: earth, fire, air, and water. He was the last Greek philosopher known to write in verse. According to the Greek biographer Diogenes Laërtius, to prove his immortality Empedocles threw himself into the Etna crater. In return Etna threw back his bronze sandal (deceit revealed). A large underwater volcano discovered near Sicily in 2006 now bears his name.

To disappear

Bruno Pontecorvo, a prominent nuclear physicist who had worked on the world's first nuclear reactor using heavy water as a neutron moderator, became a British citizen in 1948. Together with his wife and three sons, he disappeared without trace while on a camping holiday in Italy in 1950, only to turn up five years later in Russia. Pontecorvo's son Gil recalled the moment when the family abandoned all their belongings and with two KGB minders flew from Rome to Moscow via Stockholm and Helsinki: "I knew something was up because in Helsinki my father was in the trunk of the car," he said. What was up was that the British double agent Kim Philby had informed the Russians of an FBI investigation into Pontecorvo's communist sympathies. The scientist was suspected of passing on classified atomic information.

To tour efficiently

Jean-Baptiste Colbert (1619–1683), Louis XIV's esteemed controller general of finance, applied an extreme economy and a rational distribution of time to his proposed itinerary for his son's tour of Italy (published in 1699).

Rome he rated as an eight-day city, potentially stretched to eight more days if it was Holy Week. Naples and surrounds could be done in three days, while Venice, Mantua, and Turin each merited two to three days. Poor Genoa and Florence were only two-day cities, while Ravenna, Rimini, or Turin could each, according to the strict parent, be assimilated in half a day at a trot.

Castel Gandolfo, 2022
3 × 4 ¹¹⁄₁₆" (7.5 × 12 CM)

"We have another excellent countryman at Rome who plays his cards there to admiration," James Adam wrote in 1761. "Last winter he sold no less than £5,000 worth of pictures to the English, of which every person of any knowledge is convinced he put £4,000 in his pocket." The profiteer was Thomas Jenkins (1722–1798), one of the richest and most influential Englishmen in Rome—the reward for his urbanity and duplicity. Jenkins had first arrived in the city in 1752 in the company of the Welsh landscape painter Richard Wilson. He intended to study history painting, but realizing the limits of his talent soon abandoned the endeavor to deal in antiquities (but not before fulfilling a commission for Stephen Beckingham to paint *Time Discovering Truth*—a fitting epitaph for his own reputation).

Jenkins enjoyed some notoriety from the start: "Long has he been known here for his villainies"—the Jacobite Andrew Lumisden wrote to Sir Robert Strange in 1760—"However, by consummate impudence, joined to the honorable office of spy, he gets himself recommended to many English travelers." Jenkins' dubious reputation didn't stop him from being elected to the Accademia di San Luca in January 1761, or from developing a whole host of useful contacts. The German art historian Johann Joachim Winckelmann, Clement XIII's prefect of antiquities, nominated him as the agent for the sale of a gem collection, while Cardinal Albani recommended him to the Duke of York as the most qualified guide to the sights of Rome.

After a while even the Italians twigged that their antiquities were making Jenkins rich. As the Milanese Alessandro Veri wrote to his brother Pietro in 1778, Jenkins' business went "hand in hand with the working of marble." By this he meant not only the excavation of statues, but also their creative restoration. Winckelmann wrote to the painter Henry Fuseli that Jenkins had "sold the agent of George III a Venus, with a new leg, two new arms, and even the head was that of another less beautiful Venus." Others in Rome claimed that he could conjure a complete figure from any fragment—as was clearly the case with the "Jenkins Vase," a 1.72m-tall highly decorated vase mounted on an antique well head. Adding patina with tobacco juice was another specialty, while a workshop among the ruins of the Colosseum manufactured "ancient" cameos that sold just as fast as they could be made. Jenkins' legendary sales technique extended to shedding tears when parting with a "prized" possession.

Jenkins' country retreat at Castel Gandolfo was described by Father Thorpe as "a sort of trap for rich young Englishmen prepared to spend large sums on Antiques." It was here in 1787 that Goethe encountered the "beautiful Milanese" he described in his *Italian Journey*—though the prices for the statues on display were beyond his pocket. In 1798 advancing French troops confiscated all the trappings of Jenkins' worldly success, though he still managed to escape to Florence with his gem collection. There he drafted a will disclosing that the house in Rome and the Castel Gandolfo estate were only rented. All along he had been poised to take flight—but as it turned out he only got as far as Great Yarmouth, where he died shortly after landing in England.

To discover an anti-France

Marie-Henri Beyle (1783–1842), the nineteenth-century French novelist better known under his pen name Stendhal, saw himself as an honorary Italian. The last of his three novels, *The Charterhouse of Parma*, is based on the debauched life of Alessandro Farnese, who became Pope Paul III thanks to the influence of his sister Giulia, mistress of the previous Borgia Pope ("Giulia la Bella" was immortalized as the Madonna in a painting in the pontiff's private apartments).

An indifference to morality and a love of risk also characterize the lives of the novel's hero Fabrice and his aunt Gina, the Duchessa Sanseverina. Risks are also taken in Stendhal's portrait of Parma, which in fact more closely resembles Modena. The charterhouse of the title is mentioned only on the last page, and the prison where Fabrice finds happiness sounds more like the Castel Sant'Angelo in Rome (where Alessandro Farnese was actually imprisoned as a young man, on account of an obscure family quarrel). Such shufflings and pseudonyms were a specialty of Beyle/Stendhal, whose long list of aliases also took in César Louis-Bombert, Cornichon, William Crocodile, and D. Gruffort Papera, which he used to sign a review of his own *The Red and the Black* (*Le Rouge et le Noir*). Stendhal defined his ideal reader as "a 30-year-old woman of wit and learning" and claimed that the immorality of the Italian dimension of his novel would be beyond the mental and emotional grasp of his French readership. Italy was for him a sort of fictitious anti-France.

Stendhal first came to Italy as a soldier in Napoleon's army, arriving via the St Bernard pass. In Novara, while watching a performance of the Cimarosa opera *Il matrimonio segreto*, he experienced an overwhelming sense of euphoria, writing "my life was renewed and all my disappointment with Paris was buried forever." In Milan he encountered something similar—this time the ecstasy of his first sexual experience (followed by the syphilis he contracted from his lover). A cultural overdose in the church of Santa Croce in

Florence led to "a fierce palpitation of the heart (that same symptom which, in Berlin, is referred to as an attack of the nerves)"—Freud reported feeling a similar disturbance during his first encounter with the Acropolis.

In the 1980s the Italian psychiatrist Graziella Magherini made a specialty of treating foreign tourists in Florence suffering hallucinations, guilt, fainting, and an awareness of their own insignificance induced by an overwhelming cultural experience. (The majority of her patients were between the ages of 26 and 40, single and from North America or northern Europe; more than 50 percent had a previous history of psychiatric treatment.) In 1989 she released a book about this loss of self-cohesion, titled *La Sindrome di Stendhal*.

To flee England out of embarrassment

In 1575 a bout of wind prompted an embarrassed Edward de Vere, 17th Earl of Oxford (1550–1604) to flee England for Italy. According to John Aubrey, the Earl, "making of his low obeisance to Elizabeth I, happened to let a Fart, at which he was so abashed and ashamed that he went to Travell, 7 yeares."

Grey-Eyed Englishman, after Titian, *Portrait of a Young Englishman*, 2021
$3\frac{5}{16} \times 2\frac{13}{32}$" (8.5 × 6 CM)

In Sicily, however, Oxford soon gained an unrivalled chivalrous reputation. The former galley-slave Edward Webbe writes in *Rare and Most Wonderful Things* (1590) that during the French Wars of Religion, Oxford challenged anyone with any weapon to fight "in the defence of his Prince and countrey: for which he was verie highly commended, and yet no man durst be so hardie to encounter with him, so that al Italy over, he is acknowledged ever since for the same, the onely Chivallier and Noble man of England." Oxford was so influenced and enthralled by Italian culture that on returning to London he was known as the Italian Earl and, Aubrey writes, the Queen welcomed him by saying, "My Lord, I had forgott the Fart." At court Oxford introduced a number of Renaissance fashions such as embroidered and perfumed gloves. Elizabeth I's were scented with what was known as the "Earl of Oxford's perfume."

To qualify as a member
of the Society of Dilettanti

In 1734 a group of aristocrats wishing to enact the conviviality of the Grand Tour formed a London dining club known as the Society of Dilettanti. Their ostensible aim was to improve the taste of their countrymen by redirecting it along classical lines, but this was hardly a sober mission: "*Serialudo!*," went their drinking toast—"be playful about serious things." Horace Walpole (not a member) described it as a club for which "the nominal qualification is having been to Italy, and the real one, being drunk; the two chiefs are Lord Middlesex and Sir Francis Dashwood, who were seldom sober the whole time they were in Italy." In a 1740s portrait by George Knapton, Dashwood—also host of a "rigorously pagan" (Walpole again) Hellfire Club in a cave in West Wycombe—is shown dressed as a monk, worshipping the body of Venus de Milo. Middlesex, in turn, is depicted as a Roman consul in a portrait by Ferdinand Richter now hanging at Knole. A great patron of Italian opera, Middlesex was reported to have returned to England from one of his tours with "three Italian ladies for his own private use," though these ladies may have been vocalists. Besides promoting opera, society members also found time to be enlightened patrons of art and archaeology, and to spearhead the foundation of the Royal Academy. They sponsored research into the classical world—in fact they still do, sending annual donations to the British Schools in Rome and Athens. Still today, the Dilettanti gather for formal dinners around a table where the centerpiece is a mid-eighteenth-century carved chest known as the Tomb of Bacchus. Its 60 members—still elected by secret ballot—now include David Hockney.

To walk a dog

Dr James Hays, Bear-leader, after Pier Leone Ghezzi, 2014
2 × 1¹⁹⁄₃₂" (5 × 4 CM)

Lord William Gordon (1744–1825) ruined his reputation by eloping with his first cousin, Lady Sarah Bunbury, "a society beauty" who happened to be already married. A 1763–65 portrait by Sir Joshua Reynolds depicts Lady Sarah dressed in something like a Roman stola, offering a libation to the Three Graces, mythical companions of Venus. The luster of the Goddess of Love seems to have worn off after the elopement, however, and Gordon soon abandoned his paramour. Endeavoring to start afresh, he left England in 1770, announcing his intention to walk to Italy with "no other companion than a very big dog." This may have been the same "*Gordon uffziale inghlise*" who the *Tuscan Gazette* noted was in Florence in 1774, accompanying Charles Edward Stuart, the by now not so Young Pretender. Such a sighting is however perhaps unlikely, given the Catholic-crushing activities of both his brother, Lord George Gordon, and his uncle, General William Gordon of Fyvie, whom the mawkish flatterer Pompeo Batoni painted in 1765 against the backdrop of the Colosseum, wearing billowing tartans in the manner of a Roman toga.

To send home melon and broccoli seeds

"I am in high spirits at the thought of seeing Italy in so short a time, ever since I can remember I have been wishing to go into a country, where my fondness for painting and antiquities will be so indulged." This was the 19-year-old George Harcourt, Viscount Nuneham, writing to his sister in 1755 midway through a two-year tour in the company of his friend, George Bussy, Viscount Villiers, and Villiers' tutor, the poet William Whitehead. Despite his professed fondness for art, Nuneham bought little, except for the melon and broccoli seeds he sent home to his family. But he did not return to England completely empty-handed. In his luggage was a "studio" of ancient and modern marbles—small square pieces for making "the prettiest tables in the world," for which he had paid three guineas.

To join the crowd

In 1784 Sir John Fleming Leicester wrote from Rome "the town is perfectly filled with English," and in 1788 John Hawkins noted "one hundred and seventeen English travelers of fashion are now in this city."

Selected Marbles, 1996

$3\,^{15}/_{16} \times 3\,^{15}/_{16}$" (10 × 10 CM)

To be seduced (or not)

"We have very hot air today that incapacitates one to do anything," Thomas Pelham (1756–1826) wrote from Rome on August 9, 1777, perhaps in an effort to reassure his mother, who had warned him as he set off on his Grand Tour of "the trials and temptations of all sorts in a world of vice, dissipation and luxury ... How much you will be invited to depart from the paths of virtue and religion in which you have hitherto walked." His mother had cause to be worried. She knew that as a young tourist in Italy her husband, his father, had been the lover—the *cavaliere servente* or *cicisbeo*—of the married Countess Acciaioli. Hot or not, Thomas still managed to busy himself with lessons on dancing and perspective in Turin and with the purchase of a number of paintings and antiques, advised by the German painter Anton Raphael Mengs. For these transactions he carried letters from his bank in London, C. Hoare & Co, to correspondents in Turin, Milan, Rome, and Naples, all of which gave credit up to £200— a trans-European financial network that relied on bankers being men of integrity whose promise to pay was as good as money. When Thomas came to the epicenter of Italian banking, the long-serving British resident in Florence, Sir Horace Mann, introduced him to the Countess Acciaioli, his father's mistress a generation before.

To reduce barbarism
and awaken taste in Hanover

Georg Christian August Kestner (1777–1853) studied law in Göttingen, but was always destined for greater things. His mother, after all, was Charlotte Buff, who broke Goethe's heart and was the model for the character of Lotte in *The Sorrows of Young Werther*. His father, Johann—the man chosen over the 23-year-old Goethe—was a diplomat and art collector. Following his father into the civil service, Kestner was swiftly promoted, moving in 1817 from the chancellery at Hanover to the Vatican, where he was first an envoy of the Hanoverian king, then *chargé d'affaires* (for the British as well, for an extra 100 Thaler a year), before being appointed ambassador to Naples in 1834.

The posting to Italy allowed Kestner ample scope to pursue his true passion—art. Soon after his arrival in Rome he published, anonymously, a critique of the move to make Greek antiquity the basis of a "new German religious-patriotic art"—a development championed, notably, by Goethe; for Kestner, the Italian quattrocento was a more fitting model for modern painting. Alongside his regular contributions to art criticism, he found time to excavate Etruscan ruins and to co-found the Deutsche Archäologische Institut in Rome. He also dabbled in painting. In a letter to his sister in 1836 he describes being allowed to copy a portrait by Titian of Philip II (he had helped broker its sale to an Irishman). He seems quite satisfied with the results: "At a distance of two paces it looks like the original." Of course, he also amassed a huge private art collection of his own— almost 1,000 pieces, including Egyptian, Etruscan, and Greek antiquities, books, and paintings. In 1834 he wrote to his nephew Hermann that he had purchased a "painting of a girl by Raphael, a Perugino and a Leonardo da Vinci"—the latter, which eventually proved to be Pontormo's *The Penitence of St Jerome*, occupied pride of place in Kestner's apartment in the Palazzo Tomati near the Spanish Steps. Following Kestner's death in Rome in 1853, his niece Wilhelmina and great nephew George Leaves documented this salon in watercolor. The center of the image focuses on a curious high-backed sofa (a stand-in for the absent collector) on which lies a print of antique ruins, seemingly abandoned in haste.

Kestner's collection, bequeathed to his nephew Hermann, was donated in the late 1880s to the city of Hanover, which in return constructed the Kestner Museum in Renaissance style, designed

Kestner Apartment, Rome and Kestner Museum, Hanover, 2012
$2\frac{3}{4} \times 6\frac{11}{16}$" (7 × 17 CM)

by the architect Wilhelm Manchot. In the building's sky-lit second floor salon, the principal works of the collection were arranged in a sequence resembling that of the Rome apartment. To maintain the verisimilitude, the center of the room was occupied by another high-backed sofa, big brother to its Roman precedent. Kestner's nephew stipulated that the museum be open to the public, free of charge, for three days a week, and a sizeable audience duly arrived, responding to an ambition Kestner had first articulated in an 1819 letter to his sister: "Perhaps we can reduce barbarism and awaken taste in Hanover."

To rebuild Herculaneum in Malibu

The Getty Villa at 17985 Pacific Coast Highway is a Californian rendition of the Roman Villa dei Papiri discovered at Herculaneum in the mid-eighteenth century. The original, preserved for nearly 2,000 years by a 20m layer of concrete-like volcanic ash and mud, was excavated between 1750 and 1765 by the Swiss archaeologist and military engineer Karl Weber, whose methodical and systematic approach earned praise from Winckelmann—though unfortunately for Weber toxic gasses necessitated the closing of the tunnels he had built to access the ruins.

Herculaneum in Malibu, 2015
$3^{15}/_{16} \times 4^{21}/_{64}$" (10 × 11 CM)

Getty Villa, Malibu, 2015
4 $^{21}/_{64}$ × 5 $^{1}/_{2}$" (11 × 14 CM)

About 250 years later, in an attempt to win cultural recognition, the American oil tycoon J. Paul Getty heavily invested in ancient statuary, although little attention was paid to the provenance of his collection, assembled through the international antiques market during a boom time for plunderers. Getty built a gallery adjacent to his Malibu residence to house his treasures. When he ran out of space he set out to construct a Villa dei Papiri of his own further down the hill. As the original was then not completely excavated, the basic plan was sketched from Weber's 1750s drawings with additional free interpretations of antique buildings in Pompeii. Unlike the original, the Getty Villa is built over a basement parking level, its collection of Greek, Roman, and Etruscan artifacts viewed against a neo-Roman peristyle backdrop. Getty died in 1976, two years after the villa's completion, but he never managed to see it for himself. The fact that the Roman transplant could not be expanded necessitated a second site, the all-white Richard Meier-designed Getty Center, built in the hills of Los Angeles and completed in 1997.

Today, more than 80 statues excavated from the Villa dei Papiri—now generally believed to have been owned by Julius Caesar's father-in-law, Lucius Calpurnius Piso Caesoninus, can be seen at the National Archaeological Museum in Naples, along with the 1,800 papyrus scrolls for which the villa is named. Carbonized by the heat of the eruption of Vesuvius, they are inscribed with the writings of Epicurus and followers. Early attempts to decipher some resulted in their destruction, but more recently, philological analysis with the aid of microphotography has been carried out by the National Library in Naples, Utah's Brigham Young University, and UCLA. Meanwhile digital excavation of the Getty Villa presents the chance to purchase a Julius Caesar T-Shirt for $25, a Roman Mosaic Woman's T-Shirt for $22.95, or a pair of Roman Erotic Mosaic Boxer Shorts for $15.99.

To graduate from California's thunderbird carport elysium to the real thing

The high priest of the Californian steel-frame house, aka the Californian Mies, was born Jon Nelson Burk in 1922. After being discharged from the US Army Air Corps in 1946 he and his brother Cleve set up a building contractor's office with wartime friends, the Marzicola brothers. The name of the firm, "Craig Ellwood," was taken from the liquor store opposite. Five years later, Case Study House #16 (Salzman House) was heavily publicized in John Entenza's *Arts and Architecture*. By then, Jon had legally changed his name to Craig Ellwood and established his own firm, Craig Ellwood Design. In 1977 Ellwood retired to Italy. He devoted himself to painting and restoring a fifteenth-century farmhouse in the small town of Pergine Valdarno near Florence, where he lived until his death in 1992.

Craig Ellwood, Daphne House, Hillsborough, 2014
2 × 3" (5 × 7.5 CM)

To find out what the end of time looked like in 1305

Angel Rolling Up the Heavens, after Giotto,
The Last Judgement, Scrovegni Chapel, Padua, 2022
$2^{11}/_{64} \times 1^{49}/_{64}$" (5.5 × 4.5 CM)

Walter Benjamin defined three modes of time: "Circular Time," that of the seasons that repeat each year; "Linear Time," that of progress (Kant's *fortschritt*), an ever-advancing frontier; and "Apocalyptic Time," the end of time itself. One reason for traveling to Italy might be to see how this last mode of time looked in 1305. This is the year in which Giotto completed his depiction of the *Life of Christ and the Life of the Virgin* on the walls of the Scrovegni Chapel in Padua — a cycle of frescos that ends with *The Last Judgement*, which fills the space around and between a tripartite window set within the chapel's rear facade. Here, above an alarming representation of hell alongside a more benign heaven, Giotto presents two angels who step out, their feet sinking in cloud, and roll up the painted night sky like a carpet (TIME, GENTLEMEN, PLEASE, SHOW'S OVER!). This celestial rolling-up reveals the wall behind, on which Giotto painted the gates of a heavenly Jerusalem studded with precious stones—a conceptually adroit trick that may just be a self-referential Giotto unmasking the fictiveness of his painting by revealing the wall of the church for which he was also possibly architect.

To be the first to travel to Italy and to then get home

The Villa Malaparte has no equivalent in Homer's *Odyssey* narrative, except perhaps as the deck of Ulysses' ship, which he loses after negotiating the Siren Islands and surviving the maelstrom. He spends the next seven years on the island of Ogygia under the spell of the immortal nymph Calypso. A painting by Arnold Böcklin (1881), now hanging in the Kunstmuseum in Basel, shows the pair: suffering and homesick, a shrouded Ulysses scans the horizon, his back turned to the naked seductress as she sprawls out on the rocks. The scene is a psychogram of strained relations, with a setting closer to "a sea cave where nymphs had chairs of rock and sanded floors"—Homer's description of the grotto where Ulysses and crew slaughtered Helios' cattle—than Calypso's actual domestic arrangements, which were somewhat more commodious:

Upon her hearthstone a great fire blazing
scented the farthest shores with cedar smoke
and smoke of thyme, and singing high and low
in her sweet voice, before her loom a-weaving,
she passed her golden shuttle to and fro...
... Even a god who found this place
would gaze, and feel his heart beat with delight.

The home of the nymph, it seems, offers abundance, a Vitruvian *commoditas* found in neither Böcklin nor the sculptured stronghold of the Villa Malaparte. This counterpole, an alternative and sensuous mode of habitation, was the theme of the one-time Capri resident

Scenes from *Le Mépris*, 2014
$4^{11}/_{16} \times 1^{3}/_{16}$" (12 × 3 CM)

Bernard Rudofsky. Indeed, the lushness of Calypso's cave would not be out of place in his 1964 book and MoMA exhibition *Architecture Without Architects*, a milestone in the erosion of a narrowly defined functionalist hegemony. Rudofsky championed the Mediterranean lifestyle, which was, he considered, the only healthy and honest version of a modernist aesthetic, not to mention an earthy alternative to northern abstraction. In 1937 *Domus* published Rudofsky's and Luigi Cosenza's design for the Villa Campanella in Positano: two cubic masses balanced on rocky cliffs high above the sea and joined by a canopy roof. This was a condensed version of a larger cliff hanging house—the Casa Oro—which the pair built in 1935. A simultaneously traditional and modern chain of Mediterranean white box volumes and terraces (embellished, in the rendering, with elegant women leaning out over the handrails), the house seemed to grow out of the Neapolitan coast. Then, in 1938, *Domus* published Rudofksy's design for a house on the island of Procida. This was the same month that Adalberto Libera submitted the initial site plan—titled "*Progetto di Villetta di Proprietà del Sig Curzio Malaparte*"—for a building permit in nearby Capri, which was "granted quickly and discreetly through an influential intervention," according to Libera's biographers. The approved design specified an elongated rectangular building with a rusticated base and upper living room at the outer end of the roof terrace. Perhaps Libera was distracted by the construction of the Palazzo dei Congressi (he had won the prestigious 1937 competition), or his assertive client stepped in with disputed additions—like the tapering staircase similar to the one leading up to the Church of Annunziata on Lipari, where Malaparte was photographed while in exile. In either case, work progressed slowly and may or may not have been influenced by Rudofsky's published designs.

A gender-specific dialectic pairs these built and unbuilt manifestos. The harsh metaphysical poetry of the male egoist clifftop villa finds its counter in the commodious house designed by Rudofsky for his future wife, Berta Doctor. Both mediate between an idealized occupant and the world, metaphorically using geometry to locate a microcosm of the specific, of individual experience within the macrocosm.

The windows of Casa Malaparte, with their views of the majestic Faraglioni rocks, invoke a surreal sense of vertigo. Large-format glass rectangles (today's signature of Swissness) conjure both danger and refuge, imprisoning the cast of *Le Mépris* fluttering before them, caging them within their cinematically prescribed roles. Conversely, Rudofsky's house argues for the Pompeiian format—a string of rooms arranged around an open central atrium. Such a composition prioritizes a sensuality not dissimilar to that of Calypso's cave. Here the theme of movement centers on daily domestic trajectories. "*Questa è una casa di campagna per una donna senza pregiudizi,*" he wrote in *Domus* (it is a house for an open-minded woman). With this in mind the plan rescripts familiar functional codes, not only depicting the more typical infill of poché but also—through the radical and unconventional graphic intervention of sketched allegorical figures—choreographing each room.

After Arnold Böcklin, *Odysseus and Calypso*, 2014
$1^{49}/_{64} \times 2^{3}/_{4}$" (4.5 × 7 CM)

In the dining room that opens onto the courtyard, guests donning laurel wreaths and covered only from the waist down delight in an abundance of food and soft furnishings. A doorway leads to a music room where Pegasus and a Perseus-type recline against a grand piano.

House for an Independent Woman, after Bernard Rudofsky, 2014
4 $\frac{21}{64}$ × 3 $\frac{15}{16}$" (11 × 10 CM)

Now the plan comes to represent both the physical structure for living and the template for a sensuous Mediterranean lifestyle. The isometric color illustration Rudofsky produced of this arrangement is one of the most iconic images of Mediterranean modernism, advocating an epicurean and sensual way of living. Outside, a dog lies next to the lady of the house as she relaxes in a hammock. Another woman with fiery hair rides bareback across the sands of the adjacent beach.

Gio Ponti, who provided Rudofsky with his *Domus* platform, wrote that "the Mediterranean taught Rudofsky and Rudofsky taught me." In 1938 the two collaborated on the design for the San Michele Hotel, a cluster of houses and rooms scattered over a precipitous cliff on the island of Capri, with paths—leading from the room of the angels, the room of the doves, the room of the sirens, etc.—converging at the village center. On arriving guests leave their clothes in a closet and are equipped with sandals, hats, and other necessaries designed by the architects.

According to Rudofsky, a house is a commodious description of body functions, habits, behavioral patterns, and objects. In his work the DNA of the Mediterranean house is irrefutably anchored in the "techne" of doing, of making, and of dwelling. "Homes should be a cultural refuge," he argued. They are "the aesthetic backdrop for our passions." After Ulysses' odyssey, horizon-scanning windows seem less than necessary. There is no further "elsewhere." The goal is the house, the olive-stump bed. And it is here that we discover dwellings that above all else prioritize the character and sensuality of their occupants, whether Penelope, Calypso, or Berta Doctor.

To see with the eye of the lynx

Giovanni Faber—born Johannes Faber in Bamberg in 1574—traveled to Rome in 1599, soon after completing his medical studies in Würzburg. He quickly became enmeshed in the city's scientific circles, as a surgeon at the Hospital Santo Spirito in Sassia, as director of the Vatican's Botanic

Gardens and as professor for botany and medicine at the University of Rome. On April 14, 1611 he was part of a learned group who listened to Galileo Galilei present his research in astronomy—a show and tell, where the entire night was spent observing the planets through Galileo's newly invented telescope. 1611 was also the year in which both Galileo and Faber were inducted into an exclusive institute devoted to the pursuit of science, the Accademia dei Lincei—the name chosen for the sharp-eyed lynx, which according to medieval bestiaries had the power to see through rock and walls (like Superman, with his X-ray vision). The two men became close friends. Faber defended Galileo when he got into an unpleasant dispute with the German Jesuit mathematician Christoph Scheiner over the nature of sunspots (which Scheiner objected to, as a presumed blot on the perfection of the heavens). When Pope Paul V clamped down on Galileo's propagation of the Copernican theory—namely that the Sun, rather than the Earth, was the center of the cosmos—Faber, by now secretary of the Accademia, proclaimed the Linceans' support for academic freedom. And when Galileo came up with another invention which he called the *occhiolino*, "little eye," it was Faber who supplied the more enduring name of "microscope."

Faber was also a collector. While he did not command the financial means to rival great collections like the *Wunderkammer* of Rudolf II in Prague, he nevertheless had an anatomical theater and a cabinet of curiosities installed in his house near the Pantheon. Among the treasures in Faber's cabinet were skeletons of rabbits, geese, turkeys, and a hedgehog that he himself had dissected. Such collections juxtaposed the scientific and the mythological, represented by relics, medals, and anecdotal curiosities. Making use of Galileo's "little eye," Faber assured his allegiance to the world of science with his microscopic study of insects and a commentary to the *Tesoro messicano* (*Flora, Fauna and Mineralogy of Mexico*), although even here the mythological raised its head (in fact two heads) in the form of the fantastic *Amphisbaena* snake, which many years later would resurface in Jorge Luis Borges' *The Book of Imaginary Beings*.

To experience a perverse stimulation

The Marquis de Sade (1740–1814) was twice in Italy, both times on the run. In 1772 it was to avoid a sentence relating to an orgy he had organized in Marseille: he had been overgenerous with the aphrodisiacs and three of the five ladies involved had died. In 1775, after another orgy with two very young girls, Sade was back again, traveling incognito—an unnecessary precaution, as French spies reported his every move. The truant Marquis used this temporary exile as an opportunity to exercise his writing talents in the form of a travelogue, a genre he continued to pursue while imprisoned back in France. His stated aim was to write as a "perfect moralist," since his task was to speak not of himself, but only of the inhabitants of the foreign land. The resulting work was monumentally conventional—"a sea of banalities," concludes the art historian Roberto Zapperi, displaying a "crass ignorance" of the manners and ethics of Italy. Sade declared that he found *castrati* monstrous and was outraged that women could love them. However, his perversion found a subject to warm to, in Stefano Maderno's statue of the martyred St Cecilia, which expressively depicts the corpse of a young Roman girl with three sword wounds in her neck.

Aureli's St. Cecilia—Sade's Favorite, 2014
2¾ × 4½" (7 × 11.5 CM)

According to legend, Cecilia lived for three days after being dealt the mortal blows and, in her transitional state, asked the pope to build a church on the site of her home in Trastevere. Some 700 years later, in the ninth century, another pope—Paschal I—interred her "remains" in the church. In 1599 a white marble sarcophagus containing a well-preserved cypress coffin was unearthed during building renovations. Inside, lo and behold, was the shrouded, uncorrupted body of the early Christian martyr. The open coffin, a religious sensation, was put on public display, drawing crowds of ecstatic believers. Pope Clemens VIII was quick to respond. He had the coffin sealed and encased in silver, and commissioned Maderno to replicate in white marble the slumped figure exactly as it had been revealed, lying on its side shrouded in exquisitely wrinkled fabric. The face of the young, delicate and, as Sade projected, beautiful girl turns away to meet the marble slab on which she lies, revealing a neck wound with drops of marble blood.

Sade, who in any case found it difficult to distinguish between agony and ecstasy, experienced a perverse stimulation from the slumped figure. Its beauty was for him in no way diminished by the violent death it portrayed; rather, this elevated the experience to a higher level of eroticism. As the Marquis wrote, "Her soft hands are open, only a few fingers folded as if from a sudden death cramp … an impressive truth rules this heavenly work, one cannot view it without being moved... But please excuse my insistence on this subject, my taste and empathy are only those of a second-rate art lover."

To make the Pope laugh

As a thank you for Pope Sixtus V's support in a succession dispute the Polish King Sigismund III Vasa dispatched Dwarf Adam to Rome in 1588. But Sixtus's own successor, Clemens VIII, busy with his campaign to reform Roman morals, took some time to decide if he had need of a jester. Adam, now operating under the stage name

Trulla (Latin for "chamberpot") was parked in the court of Cardinal Cinzio, where his antics and bad influence almost prompted the dispatching home of two German princes, sons of William V, Duke of Bavaria. His jokes were bad but not obscene, his singing tuneless, his lute-playing tiresome.

Although never an official member of Clemens VIII's household, Trulla accompanied the Pope at various functions and outings. When asked by the Pope how many commandments there were, the little wag answered 11. Pressed as to what the eleventh might be, he answered "Thou shalt pay thy rent." The Pontiff could obviously take a hint and handed over 38 scudi. He also promised Adam a doctorate on account of his proficiency in Latin, and packed him off in a pompous procession to the University of Rome. This time the joke was on the dwarf, as no one at the university was expecting him. By now the Pontiff was becoming fond of his jester, a fondness he expressed by having two frogs put in Adam's room, knowing that the little fellow suffered from frog phobia. Before his death in 1605 Clemens VIII had the brothers Cherubino and Giovanni Alberti paint Dwarf Adam into a fresco in the Vatican's Sala Clementina.

To convince oneself that nature is always superior to art

The English painter George Stubbs (1724–1806) visited Italy in 1754, at the age of 30, "to convince himself that nature was and always is superior to art, whether Greek or Roman, and having renewed this conviction he immediately resolved upon returning home"—or so he told the artist Ozias Humphry some 40 years after the event. Stubbs' early experience of horse anatomy, gained assisting his Liverpool father as currier and leather merchant, was the foundation for a scientific gaze that would make him England's most celebrated painter of horses. After his return from Italy he spent 18 months in the smelly business of dissecting horses. The resulting drawings, now in the collection of the Royal Academy, were published in 1756 as *Anatomy of the Horse*. Humphry also reported that "it does not appear that whilst [Stubbs] resided in Rome he ever copied one picture or ever design'd one subject from an Historical Composition, nor did he make one drawing or Model from the Antique." Stubbs told Humphry that in Rome he found William Chambers, Richard Wilson, and Gavin Hamilton (who had in fact absented himself from the city between 1750 and 1756). He certainly made the acquaintance of many future clients there, but claimed always to be differing in opinion from the fellow travelers with whom he visited the collections and sights. It has been suggested that the large marble of a "Lion attacking a Horse" at the Palazzo dei Conservatori in Rome may well be the origin of Stubbs' passion for that particular theme, to which he obsessively returned throughout his painting career.

After George Stubbs, *Horse Attacked by a Lion*, 2022
2¾ × 3½" (7 × 9 CM)

To invent Nordic neoclassicism
and a birthday

Corpulent Swedish artist Johan Tobias Sergel (1740–1814), tormented by gout and rheumatism, limped buoyantly through Rome on crutches. "The air in Rome is unique, the breath of life to an artist's soul," he advised young artists, whereas "all the Nordic countries are graves to artistic genius." But back to Sweden he had to go in 1778, on the orders of Gustav III. He would return to Rome in 1783–84 as companion to the king, assisting with his purchases while falling under the spell of Canova's neoclassicism. Danish sculptor Johannes Wiedewelt (1713–1802) was in Rome in 1754, and traveled to Herculaneum with Johann Joachim Winckelmann (1717–1786). Wiedewelt's *Thoughts Concerning Taste in the Arts* of 1762 advocated the imitation of antiquity as the way to "pure taste." Another Dane, Bertel Thorvaldsen (1770–1844), would spend 40 years in Rome, always celebrating the day of his arrival—March 8, 1797—as his "Roman birthday." Acknowledged as Europe's leading sculptor (after the death of Canova), his workshop was an essential stop on the itinerary of connoisseurs. A frieze on the facade of the Thorvaldsen Museum in Copenhagen—built specially to house his work—depicts his celebrated sculptures being carried from a frigate to their new home, where they would become a cornerstone of Nordic neoclassicism.

To equip a Paris apartment

The French painter Nicolas Poussin (1594–1665) spent most of his career in Rome, where the Barberini and their circle were patrons of his early religious works. While the increasing classicism of his style distanced him from the Roman baroque that was emerging in the 1630s, the grand tourists' dissemination of his paintings spread his influence much further, providing an antique and allegoric template for the evolution of the English landscape garden. Poussin's late work after 1648, with its characteristic tiny distant figures, disturbances and calm, was much appreciated by his Parisian patron, the banker Jean Pointel.

After Pointel died—bankrupt—his apartments were found by his executors to be empty, except for 21 Poussins. One can well imagine these works prescribing a space—Pointel's darkness, an intense interiority—offering respite from the profanity of a life spent juggling money. Pointel could not bear to part with his paintings, yet now they are dispersed across the walls of the most prestigious museums of the world, an exploded Pointel apartment.

The posthumous inventory included factual descriptions like "another picture likewise painted on canvas three feet long and two and a half feet high without a frame, representing a landscape of at country where there are fountains and figures also by the said Poussin here estimated at the sum of two hundred livres.' Of the 21 works documented in 1665 the following can still beseen in various museum collections:

Landscape with a Storm, *c*1651 — Musée des Beaux-Arts, Rouen
Landscape with a Roman Road, 1648 — Dulwich Picture Gallery
The Finding of Moses, 1647 — Musée du Louvre, Paris
Landscape with Orpheus and Eurydice, 1650 –Musée du Louvre, Paris
The Judgement of Solomon, 1644 — Musée du Louvre, Paris
Landscape with a Man Recoiling from a Snake, late 1630s —
    Museum of Fine Arts, Montreal
Self-Portrait, 1644 — Gemäldegalerie, Berlin
Landscape with a Calm, 1650–51 — J. Paul Getty Museum, Los Angeles
Landscape with a Man Killed by a Snake, 1648 – National Gallery, London

The *catalogue raisonnée* of Poussin's works is documented in Anthony Blunt, *The Paintings of Nicolas Poussin: A Critical Catalogue* (London: Phaidon, 1966) while the final two paintings—*Calm* and *Snake*—are analyzed in depth in T. J. Clark's *The Sight of Death: An Experiment in Art Writing* (New Haven and London: Yale University Press, 2006).

Interior of Jean Pointel's Apartment, 2015

2¾ × 5³⁄₃₂" (7 × 13 CM)

To instigate the "bamboccianti" (large baby) style

After Pieter van Laer, *A Man Performing
a Painful Operation on a Woman's Tooth*, 2022
3 × 3" (7.5 × 7.5 CM)

The Haarlem-born genre painter Pieter van Laer (1599–1642) set off in 1623 for a study trip that took him eventually to Rome, where he fell in with the riotous colony of Dutch and Flemish artists known as the *Bentvueghels* (Birds of a Feather). Disregarding the contemporary preference for an idealized antique, not to mention his acquaintance with Claude Lorrain and Nicolas Poussin, he specialized in painting small, often ironic scenes of everyday Italian life (*A Man Performing a Painful Operation on a Woman's Tooth, Assault on Cow Herders, A Game of Bowls in a Roman Ruin, Thieves Gaming, Card Players in the Roman Forum, The Quack Dentist*). His playful disrespect for the heroic, combined with his own physical malformation, earned him the nickname Il Bamboccio (large baby or ragdoll). After 13 years in Rome van Laer returned to Haarlem, where he died, possibly by his own hand, in 1642. His Faustian self-portrait as a magician who has mistakenly summoned up a devil hangs in the Metropolitan Museum of Art, New York.

A journey to Italy was a rite of passage for many Dutch artists during the Eighty Years' War with Spain. Others in Rome around this time included Paul Bril (1556–1626), who arrived in 1582 and soon found prestigious patrons, rising to become director of the Accademia di San Luca. Cornelis van Poelenburch (1594–1667)—*Bentvueghels* nickname "Satyr"—came a little later, in 1617. His specialty was small landscapes, preceding the style of Claude; Charles I noticed his work, and summoned him to England. Herman van Swanevelt (1603–1665) reached Rome in 1629 and was one of the first to paint landscapes unpeopled by biblical or mythological figures. Andries Both (1612–1642), a genre painter influenced by van Laer, was joined in 1638 by his younger brother, Jan Both (1622–1665), a dedicated exponent of the style of Claude, who would continue to paint scenes bathed in a golden Mediterranean light long after returning to Utrecht in 1646.

After the 1648 Peace of Münster the arduous journey across the Alps began to seem less attractive when set against the prospects of a burgeoning Dutch Golden Age. The *Bentvueghels* would be disbanded in 1720, after Pope Clement XI banned their drunken initiation ritual, a parody of the baptism ceremony. But their work was already done. Having resisted overt religious or symbolic content in Italy, Dutch painters had brought back home the genre of landscape painting, whose seeds would blossom under the iconographic censure of Calvinism.

To saunter philosophically, for a year or so, on the other side of the Alps

In his 1768 novel, *A Sentimental Journey through France and Italy*, Laurence Sterne (1713–1768) gives three reasons for traveling:

"infirmity of the body,
imbecility of the mind,
or inevitable necessity."

While the title promises a journey through two countries, Mr Yorick—the protagonist and a loosely veiled Sterne alter-ego—is so often distracted by the incidental that the story concludes with him in a compromising situation in central France, having never made it out of the country. Sterne himself spent a year traveling through Italy, crossing the Alps on November 8, 1765 at Mont Cenis, where carriages were dismantled and carried by mules over the pass. (Yorick had bargained in Calais for a carriage that had made the crossing twice before—ie, a dodgy piece of third-hand equipment.) From Mont Cenis Sterne traveled via Turin, Milan and Parma to Florence, where he met the English representative Horace Mann, who gave him a letter of introduction to Cardinal Alessandro Albani in Rome—the Cardinal was known for his love of gambling, women, theater, literature, and the fine arts. By January he was in Naples, enjoying the hospitality of Sir William Hamilton, having "a jolly carnival of it—nothing but operas—*punchinellos*—*festinos* and masquerades." On February 3, 1766 Sterne wrote that he hoped to have "added at least ten years to my life by this journey to Italy," reporting that he spent a "laughing winter in Naples," where the air agreed with him. "I shall return very fat." He was back in England by June 1766.

Sterne's had been a copybook itinerary, a snappy rendition of the prototypical Grand Tour. However his mode for perceiving the otherness of Italy was entirely of a different cast from any of his forerunners. He was, as he had described Yorick, a Sentimental

Mont Cenis Crossing, 2014
$12^{19}/_{32} \times 9$" (32 × 23 CM)

Traveler. In the 1760s the word "sentiment" had a modish currency, implying a kind of reflection informed by emotion. In the case of Sterne, pathos, mingled with comedy, was elevated to a level of moral instruction—an emotional identification, a putting oneself into the scene, a subjectivism eclipsing the erudition of learning and the standard expectations of the classically educated prospective traveler.

To research tarantism and to plan an ideal city

Theraphosidae Tarantula, 2014
2¾ × 3⁵⁄₃₂" (7 × 8 CM)

George Berkeley (1685–1753), the Enlightenment philosopher of the immaterial, was also well versed in architecture, an interest perhaps first stimulated by a four-year tour of the Continent as a tutor to a young man. In the Vatican in 1716 he was especially impressed by the scale of Domenico Fontana's Apostolic Library, an encounter that would bear fruit for him when he returned to his post as senior fellow and librarian at Trinity College, Dublin (the interiors of the college's new library, completed between 1723 and 1733, were clearly influenced by Berkeley's Italian experience). In the 1720s Berkeley extended his foray into architecture by drawing up plans for an ideal city in the British colony of Bermuda (an enterprise that would later be marketed as *An essay towards preventing the ruin of Great Britain*). Here, a symmetrical city plan for this metropolis of the summer islands reflected the radiating streets of Rome's Piazza del Popolo, while a central and focusing church owed much to the one built by Inigo Jones in Covent Garden, and a main square featured a single Corinthian column, a trope Berkeley borrowed from the Piazza Sant'Oronzo in Lecce. Berkeley, who would rise to become Bishop of Cloyne, was perhaps the first Irishman to tour Puglia. While there he took the opportunity to research tarantism, where people would start to dance uncontrollably, go into convulsions, and tear off their clothes in the belief they had been bitten by a tarantula. Out of this epidemic of mass hysteria came the rather more sedate tarantella.

Not to become a professor

After his scholarship at Balliol was suspended on the grounds that he harbored Jacobite sympathies, the mathematician James Stirling of Garden (1692–1770) fled Oxford for Italy, where he had been promised a post by the Venetian ambassador to London. Whether he took up the job is unclear, but soon after he was offered another position—this time in the mathematics faculty in Padua, on the condition that he convert to the "Roman Obedience." He refused. While away the young scholar kept in close touch with Sir Isaac Newton, and his scientific network put him into contact with the engineer Giovanni Poleni, who consulted Stirling while he worked on developing the catenary curve. In 1722 Stirling happened upon the trade secrets of the glassmakers of Murano. Fearing for his life, he wrote to Newton, who funded his escape to Glasgow.

To cast 2,000 students
in toxic mud

From Cannaregio (*top*) to Marghera (*bottom*), 2021
$3\frac{5}{32} \times 4\frac{11}{16}$" (8 × 12 CM)

Some years ago Bolles+Wilson were in Venice, teaching a summer workshop at the IUAV, one of ten international teams researching strategies for urbanizing Marghera, the industrial complex on the landside of the Venetian lagoon, whose chimneys, chemical plants, and shipbuilding wharves were the model for some of Italo Calvino's "invisible cities." Across the lagoon, the hard-nosed realism of industrial production is in stark contrast to the atmospheric and touristic romanticism of Venice itself, where students find it increasingly difficult to find affordable accommodation. Many commute across the causeway from Mestre, a journey—as we hypothesized—that could be done more easily by *vaporetti* from Marghera.

At the outset, and not wanting to tackle the mega scales of a still functioning industry, site research identified an outer and completely empty island—Mud Island—a no-go zone of toxic sludge, dredged from the shipping channels of the lagoon, and a sort of "new-found-land" just waiting to be colonized. Its discovery established the program for our workshop, housing 2,000 pioneers, or rather students, whose architecture needed to insulate and protect them from their toxic surroundings.

Such an academic exercise engendered distrust in the abstraction of maps, prompting an exploratory expedition across the lagoon with Professor Amando dal Fabbro in his little wooden boat. From the Rialto we putt-putted through small canals, exiting Venice from behind the station into the Cannaregio quarter. Looking back one imagined the counterfactual histories haunting this corner of the city: Le Corbusier's Venice Hospital, Peter Eisenman's scattered and fragmented red cubes, even that most poetic of architecture's ghosts, John Hejduk's *Thirteen Towers of Cannaregio* (produced for the 1980 "10 Immagini per Venezia" exhibition).

Huge red-and-white striped chimneys became even more overwhelming as we arrived in Marghera, zigzagging between high-stacked container ships and a floating dry dock that had lifted another ship completely out of the water. Chunky wooden piles supported sculptural concrete houses that could have been green cousins to Aldo Rossi's floating theater. Nearing Mud Island, nature was seen to be taking over in the form of trees, and what we hoped might be the onset of detoxification. Nevertheless, nearby workmen engaged in bulldozing mud pointed us to a sign, which read ZONA DI SCARICO DEI FANGHI—PERICOLO DIVIETO D'ACCESSO. We retreated. Back at the university the 30 students got themselves very dirty making Mud Island models from non-toxic mud bucketed in from the bottom of the nearest canal. On each, habitation scenarios were rehearsed. The most convincing adopted a minimal circular plan and used a stealth strategy so as to appear like a cluster of familiar giant industrial red-and-white striped chimneys, 90m high, four students per floor.

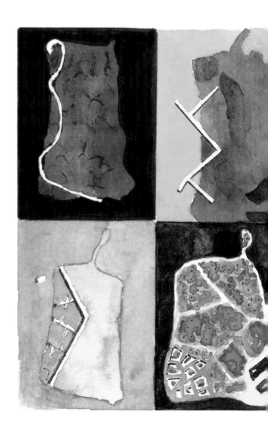

Maghera's Mud Island Settlement Options, 2021
3 5/32 × 4 11/16" (8 × 12 CM)

82

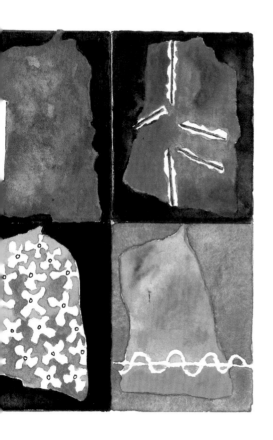

To queue

As part of a Victorian ambition aimed at "the improvement of tastes in the application of art to the production of our manufacture," the Cast Courts of the V&A Museum in South Kensington were set up to exhibit plaster facsimiles of great works for those who could not undertake their own journey to Europe. The high ceiling was most likely built to accommodate a cast of Trajan's Column, depicting the emperor's 102AD campaign against the Dacians on the Danube frontier. Unlike the original in the Roman Forum, the V&A simulacrum is lined by a brick chimney and broken into two parts (each 3.83m in diameter) for ease of viewing—"the march of the warriors of Rome will come to a sudden conclusion at the glass-ceiling, but will recommence on the floor of the court," reported *The Art Journal* when the galleries opened in 1873. A continuous frieze of low-relief figures, totaling 200m in length, spirals up the column. Many of the details that pollution has since erased from the original are today clearly legible in the cast made by the French studio of Monsieur Oudry.

Special efforts were made to attain more casts of Italian sculpture. The museum's director, Henry Cole, established an international exchange of copies of "the best works of art which each country possesses," and in 1864 a Mr Franchi, a London craftsman specializing in casts and electrotypes, was sent to Italy to make a reproduction of the Giovanni Pisano pulpit at Pisa. The result of these incentives is that the second (Italian) Cast Court, Room 46B, is overcrowded with replicas, leaving no space among the plaster heterogeneity for Trajan's cylinders, which, in a geographically confusing expedient, have landed in the middle of Room 46A, the half of the court dedicated to Spain and northern Europe.

Such discontinuities open up new possibilities within a collection. In 2010, the V&A's In-between Architecture exhibition invaded Room 46B with a plaster reproduction made by Studio Mumbai of the interior of an Indian slum dwelling, complete with a plaster tree stump

Trajan's Column, 2013
Both 5³⁄₃₂ × 5³⁄₃₂" (13 × 13 CM)

tall enough to meet the gaze of the adjacent cast of Michelangelo's *David*—an almost surreal decontextualization poignantly colliding the fruits of colonialism with an avatar of the postcolonial reality. And even Trajan's Column must withstand the assaults of cultural dislocation, as evidenced by the (overheard) response of two English schoolboys to the 2,500 spiraling figures: "Those Romans were good at queuing!," they exclaimed.

To be the subject of an equestrian painting by Uccello in Florence cathedral

The English mercenary Sir John Hawkwood, known by Niccolò Machiavelli as *Giovanni Acuto* (Cunning John), commanded the Florentine republican forces at the age of 70. When he died in Florence in 1394 he was interred in the Duomo, and Cosimo de' Medici commissioned a funerary monument to commemorate his contribution to the city. A bronze statue proving too costly, Paolo Uccello proposed a more economical solution: a painting that imitated a statue. He achieved the illusion by transferring a monochrome fresco painted in *terra verde*, the green closest to the patina of bronze, onto canvas. Uccello was obsessed by perspective construction and used the commission as an opportunity to continue his experiments with the geometricization of elements, a technique he would further explore in his portrayals of the Battle of San Romano. The Hawkwood memorial elevates mimesis to a level of abstraction in which the two-dimensional plinth and tomb project away from the canvas. Such architectonic verisimilitude is accomplished through *costruzione legittima*—the construction of a perspectival space—as well as painted lighting that mimics the actual direction of sun filtering inside the cathedral. Hawkwood's valorization in the context of the unfolding Renaissance distinguishes his trajectory from that followed by the majority of his fellow countrymen, who visited Italy to consume, rather than engage.

The Hawkwood Monument, 2013

5 3/32 × 5 3/32" (13 × 13 CM)

To track down Mario Sironi's
horses that walk on air

Equestrian Il Duce, after Mario Sironi, *Dux*, 2022
3½ × 2¾" (9 × 7 CM)

In Italy, unlike Germany, fascist propaganda was not scrubbed out in the postwar period, but simply papered over or hidden behind a curtain until such time as its artistic merits could be objectively reassessed. One case in point is the giant equestrian frescos, *Italia tra le arti e le scienze* (*Italy Among the Arts and Sciences*) produced by the artist Mario Sironi and located within Rome's Casa dei Mutilati di Guerra (Home for Wounded War Veterans, beside the Castello Sant'Angelo), a solid edifice by Marcello Piacentini, Il Duce's number one architect. Sironi, who evolved from early modernist realism, via futurism, to embrace Mussolini's fantasy of imperialism, clung to fascism to the bitter end. But unlike the also unreformed Giorgio Morandi, whose sublime still lives were widely acclaimed after the war, or the equally unapologetic fascist architect Luigi Moretti, who moved to America and built the Watergate Hotel, Sironi died disheartened, forlorn, and largely forgotten in 1961.

The two monumental equestrian frescos, each measuring almost 5 × 5m, are titled *Rex Imperator* (King Vittorio Emanuele III) and *Dux* (Mussolini). In 1946 they were covered over, with paper glued directly onto their painted surface, because of their then eclipsed militaristic ideological message (gun toting woman and *fascio littorio* toting man), and it was not until 2017 that the mural underwent a complete restoration and reappeared to the public in its original form. It is now therefore possible to see how the noble steeds each stand with one foot on the architrave of a pair of wide doors, the warm colors of which are in stark contrast to the ominous black and gray of the frescoed wall. With a metaphysical "lighter than air" touch, the horses' rear legs hover in space—an embedded *istoria* that could be interpreted as casting the voluminous, mounted Duce as a weightless blimp. In 1934, four years before the completion of the murals, aeronautics had been the decidedly modernist subject at the Milan Triennale. There the blimp theme was thematicized by Gio Ponti in the "lighter-than-air room"—filled with canvas airship models, nothing touching the floor, just like Sironi's hooves.

Gio Ponti's Lighter-than-Air Room, 2020
3½ × 3½" (9 × 9 CM)

To be dyed

Villa Poggio a Caiano with Chinese Bride, 2021
2 × 2 9/16" (5 × 6.5 CM)

At Cambridge in 1580 it was stipulated that "no scholar do wear any stuff in the outward part but black, puke [a blueish-black, inky-colored dye], or London brown." Also permitted were "other sad colors." One reason why so many English tourists ventured to Italy may have been to experience the polychromatic vivacity they were denied back home. By around 1400 fine wool from the Cotswolds was making its way to Prato's clothworkers' guilds to be dyed and woven. British wool was of a higher quality and more expensive than wool shipped from Majorca, Catalonia, or Provence. Further fueling Prato's textile industry were dyes including madder, imported from the Low Countries to make a bright red pigment, and a brassica plant known as woad, from Lombardy, which produced a deep blue and served as the foundation for other color variants—mixing the shade with madder yielded dark reds and purples. Alum from the Black Sea was used to make a mordant that set pigments onto fabric.

Rare dyes were reserved for aristocratic fabrics and included deep scarlet made from the orange-red murex shells found in the eastern Mediterranean, and vermilion, made from a crystalline substance found on the shores of the Red Sea. Today most of the workers in Prato's garment industry are Chinese (the city is home to Italy's second-largest Chinese immigrant population after Milan). When they get married many workers commemorate their wedding day by posing for photographs in front of Villa Poggio a Caiano, the retreat of the exiled Lorenzo de'Medici and accommodation for Medici brides arriving from France.

To rediscover polychromy

"Just a few days ago the author returned home from his travels in the classical land that has in every age enticed artists, because there the tender plant of art that has regularly transplanted into our less favorable region, grows on native soil." Gottfried Semper (1803–1879) couldn't wait to tell others about his trip in 1833 to Bari, Naples, and Rome. "From time to time the architect dares to share some things from his sketchbooks with the reader, whenever he believes that he is able to share something new ... an accurate mental image of antiquity in all its newness and in harmony with the conditions of its society and the southern landscape..." And what Semper wanted to share was his investigation of pigments on Trajan's Column in Rome, which suggested that the art and architecture of the ancient world was brightly colored, and far removed from Winckelmann's catalogue of white statues or Goethe's vision of "gray and white temples seen against a background of green foliage." Semper's *Preliminary Remarks on Polychrome Architecture and Sculpture in Antiquity*, published a year after his return, instead propagated a painterly architecture of trompe-l'œil. As he noted: "it has been reserved for our time to collect the still remaining traces of polychromy and establish a system that will once again reconcile antiquity with its surroundings in space and time."

To disappear between 1598 and 1603, and to import the art of the baroque masque as well as Palladianism

Inigo Jones, after Anthony van Dyck, 2010
$1^{37}\!/_{64} \times 1^{37}\!/_{64}$" (4 × 4 CM)

It is not known whether a 24-year-old Inigo Jones (1573–1652) traveled to Italy in the company of the diplomat Sir Henry Wotton (1568–1639), whose take on his own profession has been passed down through the generations: "An ambassador is an honest gentleman sent to lie abroad for the good of his country." But what is clear is that Jones disappeared from England for four or five years around 1598. His account of Stonehenge begins with the words: "Being naturally inclined in my younger years to study the arts of design" (i.e., painting and sculpture) "I passed into foreign parts" (meaning Italy) and "searched out the ruins of ancient buildings, and, returning to my native country, I applied my mind more particularly to architecture."

We might speculate that Jones learned the art of the baroque masque while working at the Medici court in Florence as an assistant to the multitalented Bernardo delle Girandole aka Buontalenti (1531–1608)—theater-master, architect, painter, sculptor, military engineer (responsible for the ideal star-shaped plan of Livorno), and inventor of the modern *gelato* (the first flavor was bergamot and orange). On returning to England, Jones brought with him Palladio's *Quattro Libri*, the first edition seen in the country. Jones's copy, dated 1601 and annotated in English and Italian, would later belong to Lord Burlington. Jones now joined the English court as a designer of theater sets and costumes and began working with the playwright Ben Jonson. In their first collaboration, *Masque of Blacknesse*, performed on Twelfth Night, 1605, the 12 daughters of Niger were introduced to Albion—the masque being performed by members of the court themselves. Many other elaborately staged plays followed, including *Masque of Beauty* (1608), with mobile temple, and the collaboration lasted until 1631, though marred by intense personal rivalry. If he needed a word to describe the greatest villain in the world, then he would call him an Inigo—Jonson once declared.

Jones's second trip to Italy (1613–14) was as an authority on all things Italian. This time he traveled with the prominent courtier Thomas Howard, 21st Earl of Arundel, patron, collector (two Holbeins, Raphael, Dürer), a friend of the natural philosopher Francis Bacon, and one of England's most influential Catholics. Together they visited Venice, Padua, Vicenza (where contact was made with Scamozzi), Bologna, and Siena, spending the winter in Rome, where Arundel gained permission to excavate statues from an ancient site. The Banqueting House, designed by Jones in 1619–22, introduced a new building typology to England, an empty, indeterminate space based on the basilica plan type—not use-specific, it could serve equally well for masques or for other formal royal receptions. The interior was composed of two stacked boxes, one with an Ionic order, the other Corinthian. The beamed ceiling had painted panels by Rubens in the manner of Vasari's Uffizi ceiling. Summerson suggests that the rusticated facade (remodeled in Portland stone in 1829 by Soane) was influenced by Giulio Romano.

The Tuscan order (which Scamozzi claimed Palladio had reconstructed—in an act of theoretical archaeology—from a Vitruvian description of Doric) appears in Jones's St Paul's church in

Covent Garden (1631), sited on the west side of the Italian piazza he had designed as part of the Bedford estate's development of "buildings fit for the habitacions of Gentlemen and men of ability." The Earl of Bedford wanted something simple: "I would have it not much better than a barn," he is alleged to have said. To which Jones quipped: "Well then, you shall have the handsomest barn in England." The Civil War interrupted this first wave of Palladian imports to England, of which the 1635 Queen's House at Greenwich is the most influential example. Jones's style of architecture was no longer politically acceptable, being too enmeshed with the old regime. And Jones himself died shortly after the execution of Charles I in 1649 — "through grief," as a contemporary put it, "for the fatal calamity of his dread master."

As a way of getting from Plymouth to London (and acquiring fame)

In 1749, when Captain Augustus Keppel put into Plymouth for repairs to his ship, the 26-year-old apprentice painter Joshua Reynolds (future RA President, Principal Painter in Ordinary to the King, and "one of the most memorable men of his time," according to a eulogy written by Edmund Burke) joined the captain on his passage to the Mediterranean. In Rome, Reynolds found himself in Piazza di Spagna, living on the third floor of the English Coffee House, enjoying the company of his compatriots, meeting prospective patrons, and drawing caricatures of the grand tourists. A dedicated student, he filled copious notebooks on his trips to Naples, Florence, Perugia, Bologna, and Venice, which served as a trove of material for future pictorial composition, including the portrait of the honorable Captain Keppel that now hangs in the National Gallery, London. In 1752 Reynolds was made a member of the Florentine Academy. That same year he returned to England with the 15-year-old Giuseppe Marchi, who remained his lifelong pupil and assistant.

To become Kentino

Of modest parentage, William Kent (1685–1748) was an apprentice at a Bridlington coach painter when a Yorkshire gentleman sponsored his trip to Italy. Kent set sail in the company of John Talman (1677–1726), a covert Catholic and dedicated antiquarian, and on arriving in Rome he studied painting under Giuseppe Chiari. There he stayed for a decisive ten years, leaving only for a tour of Naples and then two tours of northern Italy, which fueled a new enthusiasm for architecture, in particular the Palazzo del Te. To finance his time in Italy, Kent acted as an artistic advisor and "teacheroni" to wealthy Englishmen in Rome. In addition, in 1710 Sir William Wentworth agreed to pay an allowance of £40 annually (doing so for seven years) for unspecified works, while Kent's principal patron, Burrell Massingberd, paid the same sum "in ye hopes we had of your becoming a great Painter." Kent also procured art for Massingberd and others—"I have bought you a bust of Homer copy'd from ye Antique by Hercole Ferrato, it's all in order with its foot of defferent marbels—& I have bought for Sr John a bust of Paris which I think if I can get ye foot nesh'd to send ym ye next week to Leghorn."

House of William Kent, 44 Berkeley Square, London, 2013
$1^{3}/_{16} \times 2$" (3 × 5 CM)

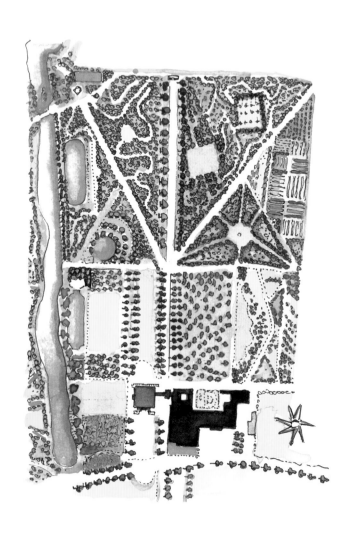

Chiswick House and William Kent's Garden, 2021
$3\,^{15}\!/_{16} \times 2\,^{3}\!/_{4}$" ($10 \times 7$ CM)

To his benefactors Kent dispatched his own drawings and copies of paintings by Correggio, Veronese, and Poussin, whose Arcadian landscapes would be embodied in his English gardens—Elysian fields designed by modeling landscapes as pictures. In his wider dealings with the English *dilettanti* Kent felt disadvantaged by his lack of education: "they make me fine promeses untill they get my drawings & then leave me so get nothing for my lose of time or for my drawing," he complained in a letter to Massingberd.

In 1719 Kent returned to England ("spending what little money I have in prints and stucco figures as heads and feet which will be of great use to me when I cannot see ye antiques") at the invitation of Lord Burlington, who had hired him to plan the gardens at Chiswick and the interior of Burlington House. ("His Lordship lik'd my designs so well both paint: & archetecture that he would make me promise at least to begin to paint for him the fierst when I come over.") Work on Rousham and Stowe gardens confirmed Kent as the foremost gardener in the English Augustinian movement. He later reveled in the self-aggrandizing nickname Kentino. Horace Walpole wrote that Kent "was a painter enough to taste the charms of landscape... He leapt the fence, and saw that all nature was a garden."

To find inspiration for the "Adam" style

Bolstered by Piranesi's assurances of his unmatched "genius for Ancient Architecture," Robert Adam set to work on his own self-promoting portfolio of antiquities "in order to instil that taste in the minds of [my] countrymen." On his way back to England in 1757 he visited Florence, surveyed Palladian villas in the Veneto and then sailed from Venice to Split, where he and his team of draftsmen—who included his tutor Clérisseau as well as Agostino Brunias and Laurent-Benoît Dewez—spent five weeks surveying the Palace of Diocletian. To convey "ideas of the magnificence" of a structure that had been encrusted and re-scripted by the encroachment of the medieval town, views of its ruined state were juxtaposed with measured reconstructions. After this excursion, Clérisseau was left at Vicenza, ostensibly to supervise the completion of the folio in Venice, but most likely to avoid outshining Adam in England. *Ruins of the Palace of the Emperor Diocletian at Spalatro in Dalmatia* would be published in London in 1764.

Adam's younger brother James (1732–1794) arrived in Rome in 1761. Like Robert, he studied under Clérisseau and continued to draw and survey ancient monuments, but with rather less enthusiasm than his brother—as his tutor couldn't help but note. Instead, he devoted a great deal of energy to amassing hundreds of pictures, drawings, antiques, and models for resale in London. With Johann Joachim Winckelmann as his intermediary, he arranged the purchase of the vast Albani collection of old master drawings for George III. (The Cardinal needed to sell in a hurry, to raise a dowry for the daughter of his liaison with Countess Cheroffini.) He also led regular reports on the progress of a project particularly dear to his brother, writing in January 1762 that "Piranesi is advancing the Campus Martius as fast as the distressed situation of his private affairs will allow him, being at present extremely distressed with the irregular conduct of his wife, who, as we say in Scotland, has been too great with another man and so he has put her in a convent for her amusement."

To start a bromance with Piranesi

While on his Grand Tour, Robert Adam (1728–1792) wrote to his family back home in Edinburgh that in Rome "I danced with all the Greatest Quality and with some of the greatest Whores and with the Handsomest of both kinds whenever I could get at them." The lucrative family business of his architect-father had provided Adam with more than enough funds to adopt the role of *Gentilhomme Anglois from one of the Ancientist Families of Scotland*, a guise that ensured contact with clients of rank and promoted his career.

"I say Piranesi old chap, one might construe that you are willfully taking license with scale!" Piranesi: "Vi aspettiamo, inglese stronzo," 2022

$5\frac{5}{16} \times 3\frac{15}{16}$" (13.5 × 10 CM)

On his arrival in Rome in 1755 Adam moved into what had been Sir Charles Hotham's rooms above the Spanish Steps and it was here, at one of the best addresses in the English quarter, that he applied himself to a regime of instruction in figures, ornament, and perspective under the tutelage of the architect Charles-Louis Clérisseau, recently expelled from the French Academy in Rome. This regime included frequent sketching expeditions, which would provide the stage for the blossoming of a special friendship: "Piranesi, who is I think the most extraordinary fellow I ever saw, is becoming immencely intimate with me," he wrote, and went on to explain why: "as he imagined at first that I was like the other English who had a love of antiques without knowledge, upon seeing some of my sketches and drawings was so highly delighted that he almost ran quite distracted and said I have more genius for the true noble architecture than any Englishman ever was in Italy." In another letter home a month later he was able to boast: "Chambers, who courted Piranesi's friendship with all the assiduity of a lover, never could bring him even to do a sketch of any one thing," whereas he "told me that whatsoever I want of him he will do for me with pleasure." Even better, Piranesi was so "satisfied" with Adam's sketches and "with the collection of antique things I have got casts of, that he has absolutely changed his resolution of dedicating his plan of ancient Rome to one of the Cardinals here and has dedicated it to me with the title of Friend and Architect Dilectantissimo nella Antichità!... It will cost me some sous in purchasing eighty or a hundred copies of it."

To engage with the Villa Malcontenta and its owners

Villa Malcontenta, 2021
$3\frac{5}{32} \times 1\frac{49}{64}$" (8 × 4.5 CM)

Antonio Foscari reports that on a trip to Venice in 1934 Le Corbusier fell into the good graces of an "exquisite" society trio whose members, Baroness Catherine d'Erlanger, Paul Rodocanachi, and Bertie Landsberg, were all at the time residents of Villa Foscari—or La Malcontenta, as it had come to be known. Landsberg, a wealthy Brazilian, had first laid eyes on the Palladian villa in 1924 and immediately initiated negotiations to buy the property. The restoration of the villa, and its guests' entertainment, quickly became his life's passion. Diaghilev's dancer Serge Lifar was a regular at La Malcontenta, as were Cecil Beaton and Anthony Blunt. Rudolf Wittkower advised on the restoration of the Veronese frescos—depicting Ovid's giants destroyed by Jupiter—which for centuries had remained hidden under a coat of whitewash. The villa was returned to original essence: when completed in the 1550s for the brothers Foscari, it was the first time the typology was not the centerpiece of a farm but a standalone retreat built for entertaining.

For Le Corbusier, Landsberg would become a valuable ally on a number of projects in Rio de Janeiro, while Baroness d'Erlanger offered to put him in touch with the industrialist Giuseppe Volpi (whose causeway, Le Corbusier commented, assured Venice's future) and tempted him with the idea of building an aquarium in Venice. This was an interesting prospect, the agile master replied, but it would be difficult to make it more beautiful than the fish of the Adriatic; a grand villa in Venice would perhaps be a more appropriate project to undertake. Writing in *Tumult and Order* (Lars Müller, 2012), La Malcontenta's current owner Antonio Foscari suggests that the 1934 visit confirmed Le Corbusier's fascination with the proportions of the villa. He would meet Landsberg again later that year, when the two returned from Rio de Janerio on the same Italian ocean liner (possibly the same trip when Le Corbusier met Josephine Baker, the subject of several nude sketches made in his hand).

In his *The Mathematics of the Ideal Villa*, Colin Rowe finds the Villa Stein at Garches—a villa merging architecture with the paintings of Léger, Braque, and Picasso—comparable in "almost" every way to La Malcontenta. "Both are blocks of corresponding volume, each measuring 8 units in length … Each house exhibits (and conceals) an alternating rhythm of double and single spatial intervals; and each house, read from front to back, displays a comparable tripartite distribution of lines of support."

To bring the circus to London

George Dance the Younger (1741–1825) visited Italy between 1759 and 1764, joining his older brother, the painter Nathaniel Dance-Holland (1735–1811), in Rome. There he met Piranesi and won the Gold Medal of the Parma Academy while studying architecture with Nicolò Giansimone.

In 1765 Dance took on his very first project, rebuilding All Hallows-on-the-Wall church, and soon after he introduced both the neoclassical crescent and the circus to London. He followed in the footsteps of his architect-father, George Dance the Elder (1695–1768), as clerk of works for the City of London, overseeing the building of Newgate Prison (designed in the mood of Piranesi's prison etchings) and St Luke's Hospital for Lunatics. As a reluctant contributor to the Royal Academy—and, eventually, the last survivor of the 40 original members—he experimented with Indian and Chinese styles before retiring to draw portraits.

To import the Campo Marzio virus

Piranesi's *Campo Marzio* folio finally appeared in 1762, replete with six pages of dedication to the "very famous" architect Robert Adam (including one inscription that makes it look like he is prematurely buried in an Appian Way tomb). James Adam immediately leapt into action, buying a "cursed number" of the plates—some £120 worth, weighing 55kg—for resale back in London. In transporting these plates—a corrosive virus, a trope of immense and destructive agency—to the metropolis, were the Adam brothers perhaps prefiguring the crewless ship of Bram Stoker's *Dracula*?

In *The Sphere and the Labyrinth* (1980) Manfredo Tafuri writes that Piranesi's *Il Campo Marzio dell'antica Roma* is both a project and a "denunciation"—a decomposition of the authority of history, of the "totality of form" and even of language itself—resulting in the denial of the city as a completed formal structure. Rather, in the *Campo Marzio,* Rome is redefined as the place of negated form—an absence of unitary structure cast by Tafuri as an "excess of visual noise," an "architectural banquet of nausea," "the triumph of the fragment," a "formless tangle of spurious organisms," a "magnetic field jammed with objects," a "semantic void." Such a characterization, Tafuri continues, explains its appeal to the English architect John Soane: "The collector, having returned to London with his Piranesi books and prints—fragments of antiquity rendered hermetic—is obliged to continue his painful journey into the labyrinth of history" and the impossibility of language. Thus did Soane reproduce a mausoleum— a prison to incarcerate himself in an architectural archaeology.

In returning to the *Campo Marzio* drawings, Tafuri also noted that "the etching commodity is not innocent"; rather, it unchains a perverse operation whereby architecture becomes a purely hedonistic game of language isolated from its sign fields. Piranesi's drawn virus encompasses an accumulation of sensation—the eighteenth-century withdrawal of the subject from things and a parallel empowerment of the subjective (the anti-metaphysical ground of experience). The clash of geometric monads sets in motion an infinitely prolonged voyage across Foucault's heterotopia—a zone with tides that undermine language and demolish syntax.

Mars-scape with Mars Rover Trajectory, 2002
$1\,^{37}\!/_{64} \times 4\,^{21}\!/_{64}$" (4 × 11 CM)

The Roman Campus Martius (Field of Mars) lay outside the ancient city walls, extending from today's Spanish Steps to the Piazza del Popolo. This was a zone originally reserved for military and recreational use, but in Imperial Rome it became the site of public pleasures. Piranesi's fictional projection of this field manifested a typical eighteenth-century typological experimentation in which actual buildings—Hadrian's Tomb, the Pantheon, or the Theater of Marcellus—were reduced to minor incidents amongst the vast geometrical deformations and exceptions constituting this topological sample book.

The linguistic crisis revealed in Tafuri's "Field of Mars" reading is echoed in a semantic infantilism that seems to have struck those NASA scientists directing the 1997 *Pathfinder* spacecraft to the surface of Mars itself—when they named the rock fragments bumped into by the exploratory Mars Rover: Yogi, Scooby Doo, Roadrunner Flats, Moe, Chimp, Big Crater, Zaphoid, Flat Top, and Twin Peaks.

To get one's teacher kicked out of the Royal Academy

On his Grand Tour of Europe from 1801 to 1805 Robert Smirke (1781–1869) took in numerous Italian cities, but as tastes began to shift to Greek revival and Napoleonic troops lurked on the peninsula, it was Greece that captured his attention. "How can I by description give you any idea of the great pleasure I enjoyed in the sight of these ancient buildings of Athens!," he wrote to his father, the painter and Royal Academician Robert Smirke Sr. "How strongly were exemplified in them the grandeur and effect of simplicity in architecture!"

Prior to his trip Smirke had spent less than a year as a pupil of John Soane. However the relationship was strained. Writing to his father, he reported that Soane found "my drawing was slovenly because it was too great a scale, my scale, also, being too long, and he finished saying the whole of it was excessively slovenly, and that I should draw it out again on the back not to waste another sheet about it." On returning from Europe, Smirke continued his training with Soane's old teacher, George Dance the Younger, and later designed the Covent Garden Opera House—the first Doric building in London. It was this building that got Soane into hot water at the Royal Academy. In his fourth lecture as professor of architecture—a position he had wrested from George Dance—Soane criticized the opera house for "sacrificing everything to one front of the building," a "glaring impropriety" that was "subversive of true taste." This impertinence caused horror in the ranks of the Academicians, with the elder Smirke heading a campaign for Soane's dismissal. A three-year stand-off followed. When the RA passed a new rule forbidding their lecturers to criticize any living artist, Soane bowed to pressure and delivered a new, sanitized version of the talk. Meanwhile, unrepentant and unrestrained, Smirke further applied his giant order across the front of the British Museum. His brother Sydney (1798–1879) was responsible for the Reading Room inside.

To put some distance between oneself and one's 13-year-old bride

To annul a gambling debt owed to the Earl of Cadogan, the 1st Duke of Richmond arranged the marriage of his 18-year-old son, Charles Lennox (1701–1750) to the earl's 13-year-old daughter Sarah. What Sarah thought of the arrangement is not recorded, but deeming his child-bride "dowdy," Charles set off on tour immediately after the wedding. It took him two years to get to Italy, and he had barely arrived when, in April 1721, he was forced to "retire some leagues from Rome ... in order to avoid any insults on account of his religion." One year later he was reunited with his wife, reportedly finding her much more attractive than before. Sometime later, he advised a friend traveling to Italy, "the Princess Pamphili is the ugliest woman in the world. Damn'd proud also, and stark staring mad, but a Devilish deal of Witt."

To receive an education

For the less prudish among the English travelers, the Italian tradition of the *cavaliere servente* or *cicisbeo*—the professed lover of a married woman who accompanied her on social occasions, including church—offered irresistible temptations. Arriving in Turin in 1760 a 20-year-old Charles Boothby Skirmisher (1740–1800, known as "Prince Boothby") adopted the custom and readily "attached himself to a very clever woman," one Madame de St Giles, at that time "near 50 years old ... who was of great service to him—she brushed him up greatly." Ever the carouser, later that year Boothby made his way to Florence, where he is depicted in Thomas Patch's *Punch Party*, now on show in Chatsworth House. Taking care not to limit his talents to one woman, he took his *cicisbeismo* quite seriously. On receiving pressing orders to return to England in February 1761, Boothby apparently left the Countess Acciaioli (previously the mistress of Thomas Pelham, the 1st Earl of Chichester) "in tears." Not for long, no doubt; ex-*cicisbei* were generally referred to as *spiantati*, "eradicated," "rooted out."

To party with Patch and Mann

Sir Horace Mann (1706–1786) was a delicate youth. Ever fearful for his health, he made his first Italian visit (1732–33) accompanied, like a proto-Dracula, by a coffin. Five years later he returned as the British representative, a post he held for almost 50 years thanks to the influence of the Walpoles—Sir Robert in the first instance, and then his nephew Horace. Mann's regular and candid correspondence with the latter Walpole provides valuable insights into the goings-on among the English on tour. His early duties included the coordination of a spy network for informing British authorities on the movements of the exiled Stuarts. But, as Edward Gibbon noted, Mann's "most serious business was that of entertaining the English." He kept open house for all of his British visitors, and *conversazioni* held at his residence

Partying with Patch and Mann, after Thomas Patch,
British Gentlemen at Sir Horace Mann's Home in Florence, 2013
3 15/16 × 5 29/32" (10 × 15 CM)

in the Palazzo Manetti were attended by "all the married ladies of fashion in Florence." Regarding his character, it was reported that "he has been so long out of England that he [has] lost the manliness of an Englishman, and has borrowed the effeminacy of Italy." His own private circle included the extremely wealthy 2nd Earl Tylney—"an unhappy man who could not resist the temptations & instigations of a passion, contrary to reason, & at which nature shudders." Another friend was painter Thomas Patch, who, like Mann, dealt in antiquities. After arriving in Rome in 1747 Patch studied under Claude-Joseph Vernet and became a member of Lord Charlemont's short-lived British Academy (he was also instrumental in its 1753 demise) but in 1755 he was banished from the city for indiscretions relating to his servant-boy Girolamo. Patch then moved to Florence and lived at the Fondaci di Santo Spirito, across the street from Mann, who grumbled, "though he does not live in my house, he is never out of it a whole day." While Patch painted a number of views of Florence and surrounds influenced by Giuseppe Zocchi, he is best remembered for his satirical caricatures of British gentlemen imbibing at Mann's table. Snoozing, pontificating, toasting, and guzzling, his tableau profiles, with exaggerated chins (or none at all), depict in fastidious detail the epicurean high points of the Grand Tour.

To verify the contents of a book

To Horace Walpole, Richard Boyle, 3rd Earl of Burlington (1694–1753), was the "Apollo of the Arts," a patron of Italian painting and opera, and a lover of architecture—a passion ignited by books. After reading *Vitruvius Britannicus* (1715) fresh off the press, Burlington dismissed the architect he had employed to refashion his townhouse in Piccadilly—the Rome-trained but much-too-baroque James Gibbs, who had added a curved colonnade around the forecourt, à la Bernini—and hired the book's author, Colen Campbell, to continue the work in a more understated style inspired by the buildings of ancient Rome. On his next journey to Italy in 1719, he made an architectural tour of the Veneto, guided by his copy of Palladio's *Quattro libri dell'architectura* and by the drawings of Inigo Jones, architect of the first neoclassical buildings in England a century before.

Possibly Palladio, after El Greco, 2010
$2^{23}\!/_{64} \times 1^{37}\!/_{64}$" (6 × 4 CM)

He returned from this tour with William Kent, who moved in with him at Burlington House and began decorating the interiors: "I made a sketch in collers for the great roome in the front, and all the rest of the ornaments yt are, to be al Italiano." Kent's first painted scheme for the new building (now above the central staircase of the Royal Academy) was a circular glorification of Inigo Jones, with a *putto* pointing to Campbell's design for the front of Burlington House. In 1726 the 3rd Earl began work on a suburban villa in Chiswick, again aided by Campbell and Kent. While some of his fellow aristocrats criticized his enthusiasm for designing, which smacked of demeaning "manual" work, Burlington did not distinguish himself by his practical nature. The house was "too small to live in, and too big to hang on a watch," according to Lord Hervey. But it was entirely successful in its more elevated role of establishing Palladianism as the house style for English aristocrats who saw themselves as Roman senators reborn.

To be miserable

Above Gibbs's mantelpiece—a window to Rome—a painting of the
Cestius Pyramid; the nearby cemetery is for non-Catholics including
Shelley and Keats. The nearest metro station is called "Piramide," 2012
2¾ × 2" (7 × 5 CM)

James Gibbs (1682–1754) began his training for the priesthood at
the Pontifical Scots College in Rome in October 1703, a path he soon
abandoned to become a pupil of the city's leading baroque architect,
Carlo Fontana. He received an education that was professional—not
to mention highly fashionable—but he did not find things easy.
Towards the end of his fourth year in Rome he wrote to his new friend,
Sir John Perceval, who had recently left the city: "When you went
away I am sorry I did not go along with you, though it had been to
carry a livery in your service, for things go so ill here, and there is such
a pack of us, and so jealous of one another, that the one would see the
other hanged." The only reason he did not beg to be taken along was
that he needed to stay a "short time longer to perfectionate myself
in this most miserable business of architecture." Later in the same
letter, Gibbs delivers more bad news, this time regarding the arrest
of Perceval's antiquary, the well-known dealer Ficarone, "for buying a
necklace of the Queen of Poland ... worth five hundred crowns, and he
bought it for one hundred. They say it will go hard with him."

Living Room of James Gibbs, 11 Henrietta Street, London,
with a Window to Rome, 2012
5 3/32 × 5 3/32" (13 × 13 CM)

To fall overboard in a white suit

Josef-Paul Kleihues as Fitzcarraldo, 1980
$3\frac{1}{2} \times 4\frac{11}{16}$" ($9 \times 12$ CM)

In 1980 the ritual of large numbers of architects trooping to Venice from all over the world was initiated with the first-ever architecture biennale. Directed by Paolo Portoghesi and titled The Presence of the Past (or "*architecture dans le boudoir*," as Manfredo Tafuri mischievously subtitled it, damning its "perfidious enchantment"), the event took place within the warehouses of the city's Arsenale. Central to the display was the transformation of the Arsenale's monumental Doric-colonnaded nave into *La Strada Novissima*, a street constructed by unemployed technicians from Rome's Cinecittà studio, along which facades by 20 bright stars in the architectural firmament briefly became neighbors (even if the conviviality of this grouping was not without internal hierarchies, as 7.2m above the main *strada* was a second level where 55 lesser-known architects "bent on preserving the tradition of architectural communication" were exhibiting their own biographical or physical "architectural self-portrait").

Among the 20 exhibitors on the ground floor were a number of Italian architects, all adjacent to each other, including Costantino

Dardi, Franco Purini, and Massimo Scolari, together with eight Americans, most of whom were the oligarchs of postmodernism—Michael Graves, Robert A. M. Stern, Charles Moore, Robert Venturi, and Stanley Tigerman—and a peppering of Europeans, Ricardo Bofill, Hans Hollein, O. M. Ungers, and Léon Krier. In addition to these eminences, one newcomer on the block was Josef-Paul Kleihues, the recently appointed director of the IBA Berlin (*Internationale Bauausstellung Berlin*). As the man charged with bestowing several major building commissions, his arrival was eagerly anticipated, and Kleihues perhaps knowingly played up the drama, arranging for his own facade to be constructed off-site and then ceremonially transported by boat to the Corderie. Kleihues himself followed on a second barge. As this vessel circumnavigated the city, the architect stood proudly midship, looking resplendent in his white suit and hat—a portent of Klaus Kinski's Fitzcarraldo transporting an opera house deep into the South American jungle. But the haughty posture of this passenger may not have been to the liking of the barge's captain, who judging by his blue artisan's jacket was likely a member of the Communist Party. At least this is one explanation as to why, as the boat neared the shore, he steered straight into the Arsenale quayside, pitching the architect unceremoniously into the canal.

To become innocent

It was, however, Aldo Rossi's entry, the *Teatro del Mondo*—Theater of the World—that made the biggest splash, and produced an image for the 1980 biennale so sustaining that it is now embossed in architecture's popular imagination. Poised majestically alongside the Fondamenta Zattere ai Saloni and facing the golden orb of the Old Customs House Tower, the yellow wood and Aegean blue trim of this floating playhouse easily eclipsed the attention-seekers of *La Strada Novissima* and for a few months recomposed the sublime spatial ensemble of the Piazza San Marco.

Rossi conceived his *teatro* as both an abstraction and a recuperation of the eighteenth-century floating theaters that once dotted the Venetian lagoon. The design was based around a large drum, octagonal in plan, which incorporated the central stage and, topped with a zinc roof, extended to a height of 25m. Around this space were adjoining side galleries which provided seating for up to 400 people. Rossi arranged for the whole composition to be assembled on a barge anchored in the nearby Fusina shipyard. Once completed it was then towed across the lagoon and opened on November 11, 1979. Buildings, according to Rossi, are like a succession of opportunities to distance oneself from the original idea. His floating theater, hyper-poetic, with an oneiric realism, nevertheless displays a prioritizing of form, artifice becoming its own domain, a built equivalent to the metaphysics of de Chirico.

Beguiled by the building, some of us who had witnessed the entrance of the *Teatro del Mondo* traveled back to Venice not long after, this time with our students in tow. But the theater had disappeared. Its ultimate tragic fate was to be towed across the Adriatic and scrapped in Dubrovnik—was it already underway? Hoping against hope, we started searching for it, even scanning the lagoon from the top of a ladder in the San Michele cemetery next to the grave of Sergei Diaghilev. A tip-off then led us to Palladio's Villa Foscari—La Malcontenta—lurking with sullen dignity behind Marghera's southern industrial canal; from there, miraculously, we could see another noble silhouette, the *teatro* itself, playing truant among the reeds on the banks of the Brenta. Stepping on board one of the students immediately tore off part of a blue-painted window frame. "Show some respect," we shrieked, "this is architecture, not the gift shop at Disneyworld." Of course, that souvenir, if she had been allowed to keep it, would now be a museum exhibit. As Rossi once wrote, "all forms become innocent somewhere between fascism and ideology."

To Encounter Aldo Rossi, 2022
3½ × 3½" (9 × 9 CM)

To get some ideas for a mausoleum

John Soane, Dulwich Picture Gallery, De-Pictured, 2012
$3\frac{1}{2} \times 5\frac{3}{32}$" (9 × 13 CM)

John Soane (1753–1837) visited Italy between 1778 and 1780. The son of a bricklayer, he trained in the offices of Henry Holland and George Dance and traveled to Italy on a scholarship awarded by the Royal Academy. In Rome he was taken up by the eccentric Frederick Augustus Hervey, Bishop of Derry, who brought him back to Ireland to design a mausoleum for his elder brother, Lord George Hervey. Soane's own family tomb, with its pendentive vault, was the template for the iconic English telephone box designed by Giles Gilbert Scott.

To solve the Tempesta

In 2012, more than 30 years after Rossi's captivating float across the Venetian lagoon, we found ourselves wandering away from the overwhelming Giardini and into the city's Gallerie dell'Accademia, where we were confronted by one of art history's great enigmas, Giorgione's *La Tempesta* (1508). The painting shows a woman sitting in a picturesque grove suckling a baby beneath a leaden sky, while a man, possibly a soldier, stands *contrapposto* on the left. But precisely what the image is conveying is unclear. Is it a pastoral Arcadia illustrating the *Hypnerotomachia*, in which the all-round Renaissance

Man Polphilo pursues his lover Polia through a dreamlike landscape, or does the scene really present Zeus, about to lightning-zap the mortal Iasion as punishment for his tryst with the goddess Demeter?

Baffled, and looking for consolation, we wandered around the corner to an Aldo Rossi retrospective at the Fondazione Vedova, located on the Zattere, a few steps from where his famous theater had been moored. Here we bumped into a room-sized model of the *Teatro del Mondo* and progressed up a gentle ramp with familiar, now canonized, drawings on our left, and analogical objects on our right — coffee pots, a copper horse, a Japanese flag. Buried in the middle of this collection of curiosities lay a life-size wooden Pinocchio. Of course, the wooden boy's composition could be read as a Rossi-esque alphabet of geometric forms, a syntactical alignment of empty signs, cones and cylinders, but in the exhibition the model was lying across the knees of another mannequin in the pose of the Pietà. And yet, as we know, Pinocchio had no mother.

Pinocchio in Rossi's Laboratory, 2012
$3\frac{3}{32} \times 5\frac{1}{2}$" (8 × 14 CM)

Two successive exhibits therefore seemed to require further investigation. Returning first to *La Tempesta*, one possible way to understand the picture was to live with it, as Gabriele Vendramin, the man who commissioned it, had done. The internet age now makes

Chinese Copy of Giorgione's *The Tempest*, Corrected, 2012
20 ⁴³⁄₆₄ × 17 ²³⁄₃₂" (52.5 × 45 CM)

such delusional aspirations possible, with a large range of analogue art suppliers, like *www.1st-art-gallery.com*, offering oil reproductions of any masterpiece, hand-painted by "certified artists" to any size or proportion. An order was immediately placed; the email went to America, but it turned out the artists were in China and were less than adept in Renaissance brushstroke technique. Once unfurled, the rolled canvas, still smelling of fresh paint, was rather underwhelming. The only solution seemed to be to make our own corrections, reworking in acrylic over the oil base, a process of direct intervention on the canvas. Very quickly, these additions became more interpretative and analytical. For instance, the rotundity of Giorgione's female implied a composition of circles (breast, infant, knee), while heavy stone objects took on a metaphysical hovering. Turning our attention to the figure on the left of the frame, the little red jacket and almost hinged posture suddenly suggested Pinocchio, and so puppet joints and a conical hat were soon added. Warming to this theme, a nasal vector then ricocheted between the painting's various actors, which immediately defined spatial relationships and even spiraled back to the distant city—*la città analoga* (with *Teatro del Mondo*). Aldo Rossi's Pinocchio as analytical tool had somehow offered a radical new geometric interpretation to the puzzle of Giorgione's *Tempesta*.

Pinocchio's Repose, 2012
$2^{11}/_{64} \times 2^{11}/_{64}$" (5.5 × 5.5 CM)

To cure hypochondria, hysteria, mania, and melancholia

Already in 1621 the Oxford University scholar Robert Burton was advancing the idea of "therapeutic travel" in his encyclopedic *Anatomy of Melancholy*. There is "no better physic for a melancholy man than change of air and variety of places, to travel abroad and see fashions," he wrote. "Every country is full of such delightsome prospects." Among these delights he particularly recommended the Italian province of Collalto, the great pyramids of Egypt, the view from Mount Sion and St Mark's "steeple" in Venice. More than a century later, Europe's healing properties were still being prescribed to England's wealthy and infirm. Lady Northumberland's gout was allegedly cured by Swiss scenery, Henry Penton's by the balmier environs of Naples and Rome. In fact, "the heat of an Italian summer" was the ideal remedy for a whole host of symptoms including consumption, hysteria, and depression. While on a Grand Tour of Italy in 1793, the notable bear-leader Thomas Brand (1751–1814) observed that "the annual flight of English, men, women, and children is prodigious and all winter round this gulph."

To draw the plates of the Roman baths and to borrow the life story of one's namesake

Like William Kent, the London-born Scot Charles Cameron (*c* 1743–1812) was not one of the "milordi" who saw Italy on a Grand Tour, but was of more humble stock. The son of a builder, he journeyed to Rome to survey the Diocletian and other Imperial Roman baths, continuing work begun by his master, the architect Isaac Ware, a protégé of Burlington. While there he may have met Charles Cameron of Lochiel, a distinguished Jacobite in the circle of Charles Edward Stuart and a connoisseur of Italian culture. On his return to England he published his studies as *The Baths of the Romans Explained and Illustrated* (1772). The book came to the attention of Catherine the Great, who wanted to recreate a little bit of antiquity of her own, a place where the "Caesars, Augustuses and Ciceros and such patrons as Maecenas" might gather. Charles-Louis Clérisseau (1721–1820) was her first choice of architect. Deciding the ideal gathering place was a bathhouse, he produced designs for a structure based on the Baths of Diocletian and larger than the whole of the existing Tsarskoye Selo Palace. Mr Cameron, who was invited to St Petersburg in 1779, offered a more practical solution, and the empress declared herself "captivated" by the architect, "by birth a Jacobite, educated in Rome...he has a wonderful mind, afire with inspiration." Part of that inspiration was perhaps to claim Cameron of Lochiel's ancestry for his own. The success of the bathhouse—which Pushkin declared the "Temple of Minerva of Rus"—marked the start of an illustrious career as an imperial architect. The Russians knew he was an aristocrat by the way he ignored the other nobles at court.

To take a course in antiques and abduct a composer

Peter Beckford of Steepleton, Dorset (1739–1811) was painted by Pompeo Batoni in Rome in 1766 while on a six-week antiquities tour. He visited "stones and rubbish of very little importance, for what? To say I had visited all the antiquaries of Rome." Unimpressed with these ancient treasures but equally uninterested in taking up the gambling habits of his peers, Beckford devoted himself to the "less ruinous" pastime of hosting musical concerts. The talent of the prodigious 14-year-old Muzio Clementi soon captured his attention. Beckford offered Muzio's silversmith father a not inconsiderable sum in exchange for permission to bring the young composer back to England, where he promised to launch his career. The arrangement was more of an abduction than patronage—Beckford reportedly used the boy for his own personal entertainment, and there is no evidence to suggest he ever provided any musical tuition. For seven years Clementi practiced the harpsichord at his patron's estate in Dorset, while Beckford himself wrote the two-volume *Familiar Letters from Italy, to a Friend in England* and a number of books about fox hunting, his real passion. When finally freed from servitude in 1774, Clementi moved to London and quickly gained a reputation as a renowned harpsichordist. Although he made a number of trips to the Continent—including a three-year European tour where he played for Marie-Antoinette and found both a friend and a rival in Wolfgang Amadeus Mozart—he would spend the rest of his life in England as a composer, music publisher and pianoforte manufacturer.

To tire of "The Cares of Pupillage and the Torment of Exile"

The Reverend Thomas Brand (1751–1814) spent nearly ten years in Italy as a bear-leader, tutoring and chaperoning young Englishmen including Lord Bruce, Thomas Duncombe of Copgrove and Sir Charles Graham—who were alternately "jolly-boys" and "very absurd riotous drunken fellows." Less equivocally, he described the royal family at Turin as "a queer set of beings and in my mind enough to disgust any man of sense." The reverend's travels on the Continent left him unimpressed by "the wonderful deficiency of good taste" in baroque architecture. The stern Doric temples of Sicily were much more to his liking.

Gavin Hamilton Leading an English Party
at the Ruins of Gabii, after Giuseppe Cades, 2013
1³⁷⁄₆₄ × 2¾" (4 × 7 CM)

To learn how Venetians deal with high water

Wading in Venice, 2012
$4^{11}/_{16} \times 1^{3}/_{16}$" (12 × 3 CM)

To reach a new "degrees of happiness"

Sir Godfrey Webster, 4th Baronet, was a compulsive gambler and deep in debt. In a bid to save his finances he married Lady Elizabeth Vassall (1771–1845), but the 15-year-old heiress was not yet ready to trace out an existence as his wife and insisted on traveling abroad, where she found a welcome freedom from domestic and social convention. Travel allowed Lady Elizabeth to make up for the deficiencies of growing up too fast. Notwithstanding the reluctant company of Sir Godfrey, who would have much preferred to stay at home, she was able to learn new languages, discuss literature, visit galleries and monuments, and take a lover (or two). She kept a detailed journal, writing that in Nice "I was left alone at 20 years old in a foreign country without a relation or any real friend, yet some of the least miserable, I might add the most happy hours, of my life were passed there. I lived with great discretion, even to prudery. I never admitted any male visitors (except to numerous dinners), either in the morning or evening, with the exception only of two—Dr Drew, and a grave married man, a Mr Cowper." Arriving at Turin, she "went out every morning to see the objects most worthy of notice, and the evening I always passed with friends who came to see me." Such company included Thomas Pelham, her husband's political advisor, with whom she began an extramarital affair. Lady Webster's daily outings instilled in her an affinity for life abroad, and for Italy in particular. At Bacoli, she wrote, "The weather was delicious, truly Italian, the night serene, with just enough air to waft the fragrance of the orange flower, then in blossom. Through the leaves of the trees we caught glimpses of the trembling moonbeams on the glassy surface of the bay; all objects conspired to soothe my mind and the sensations I felt were those of ecstatic rapture. I was so happy that when I reached my bedroom, I dismissed my maid, and sat up the whole night looking from my window upon the sea."

In the introduction to her edited diaries, the Earl of Ilchester describes her reputation as "that of an imperious, downright woman, who said just what she thought, without reference to the feelings of her hearers." The same is true for her writings. In Paestum she described temples whose "appearance was majestic, but precisely what I had conceived them to be from the drawings I had seen. They are the only remains in Italy of early Grecian architecture. The Doric, to my taste is too uneven. The columns are squat and clumsy. The inhabitants are savage and ignorant." She found Salerno, "like all the goods of this life … counterbalanced by a portion of evil, as half the year it is untenable on account of the malaria." And the Marchesa Pacca, whom she met on the way to Arpaia, "was also delightful, not to the eye, for she was hideous, nor to the ear, for she squalled, nor to the nose, for she was an Italian." But even Lady Webster could not escape her own exacting words: "so old and yet so silly," she said of herself on the eve of her 23rd birthday. As she gained more knowledge of the world, her unhappiness in her "wretched marriage" became acute:

"Detestable gold!" she proclaimed when her father died, leaving her a yearly inheritance of £10,000. "What a lure for a villain, and too dearly have I become the victim to him."

But even while suffering a self-described "melancholic solitude," "her ambitions," wrote Ilchester, "could not be confined to any particular groove, and her spirit would not allow her to stoop to a position of dependence." When her "tormentor" husband returned to England in 1795 to pursue his parliamentary career, she refused to accompany him, pleading ill health (she was in the early stages of pregnancy). But "to say the truth," she told her diary, "I enjoyed myself too much here to risk the change of scene." She stayed in Italy for another year, took a house in Florence and eventually found happiness, for it was at one of the many salons she hosted that she met her future husband, Henry Holland ("Ld H")—two years her junior and "quite delightful. He is eager without rashness, well-bred without ceremony … in short he is exactly what all must like, esteem, and admire." Lady Webster's marriage to Sir Godfrey was annulled on July 4, 1797. "On the fifth I signed a deed by which I made over my whole fortune to Sir G. W., for our joint lives, for the insignificant sum of 800*l.* Every mean device, every paltry chicane that could extort money from us was had recourse to." The next day she married Lord Holland, confiding "that I can scarcely figure to myself a blessing that I do not possess—indeed, the having such a companion as I have is, in itself, everything without the accessories of other advantages."

To look back once more

As Lady Holland, Lady Elizabeth would eventually return to England without complaint, but in 1793, the prospect of making the trip home with then-husband Godfrey was unbearable. "How much I detest the prospect of a residence in England, even though it be but for a few weeks; country, climate, manners, everything is odious to me." The journey was long and difficult—on the way to St Rémy she was "obliged to submit to be chucked upon a sack of wheat on a *bête-de-somme*. The muleteer considered me a bale of goods entrusted to his care to convey without damage, and so far thought of me, but not the least as to my ease or comfort." However the most painful moment was taking in a final view of Italy from the Alps. "I turned my back on Italy with regret," she recollected. "The men carried me backwards down the mountain. The snow on this side very deep, and they waded through it with great labor; they often fell, but I was neither hurt nor frightened. My intrepidity is more owing to an indifference about life than to natural courage."

To publish letters from Italy

Johann Wolfgang Goethe, 2013
1 ³⁄₁₆ × 1" (3 × 2.5 CM)

Die Hauptabsicht meiner Reise war: mich von den physisch-moralischen Übelen zu heilen, die mich in Deutschland quälten und mich zuletzt unbrauchbar machten; sodann, den heißen Durst nach wahrer Kunst zu stillen; das erste ist mir ziemlich, das letzte ganz geglückt.

The principal reason of my travels was to cure me from the physical and moral malaise that tortured me in Germany, rendering me practically useless; also to appease my great thirst for true art; the first purpose is apparently, and the second totally and happily achieved.

Briefe aus Italien 1786–1788

Johann Wolfgang Goethe (1749–1832) and the painter Johann Heinrich Wilhelm Tischbein (1751–1829) shared lodgings on the Corso in Rome. One day in 1786 Goethe wrote in his diary, "Tischbein is looking at me strangely, I think he is planning something."

One year later, Tischbein's portrait of the poet reclining like an antique river god on a fallen obelisk in the Roman Campagna was complete. "It is a fine picture, only too big (164 × 206 CM) to fit in

Goethe Fragments in the Campagna (Fractal Ruins) *et in Arcadia Ego*,
after Johann Heinrich Wilhelm Tischbein, 2008
$4\,{}^{11}\!/_{16} \times 6\,{}^{19}\!/_{64}$" (12 × 16 CM)

our northern houses," the subject later commented. The original is in Frankfurt's Städel Museum. Goethe settled for a watercolor copy (13.2 × 20.9 CM) by Friedrich Bury. But what of the Campagna after Goethe? Might not Goethe's intense gaze into antiquity also have dislodged the distant aqueduct and the cylindrical mausoleum of Caecilia Metella, launching their fractal iterations into the ether just as countless copies have carried Tischbein's composition into the global discourse of iconic images?

The Roman Campagna after Goethe (Deleted),
after Johann Heinrich Wilhelm Tischbein, 2008
$3\,^{47}\!/_{64} \times 5\,^{33}\!/_{64}$" (9.5 × 14 CM)

To look up

Dwindling funds (the consequence of an extravagant lifestyle) took Lady Anna Miller (1741–1781) and her husband to Europe as an economizing measure. The couple's travels resulted in the three-volume *Letters from Italy*, published anonymously in 1777. In dispatches to relatives and friends, the female narrator surmises that Piranesi was "amongst the first copper engravers and on a good day could be agreeable to strangers." The ceilings of the Pitti Palace by Pietro da Cortona are described as "subjects from heathen mythology, it would take a volume to explain ... they are symbolical, mysterious, I got a pain in my neck from looking up at them.'

To be plagued by Odori

"The truth is, our dear Venetians are nothing less than cleanly; St Mark's Place is all covered over in a morning with chicken-coops, which stink one to death; as nobody I believe thinks of changing their baskets." This was one of the numerous critiques made by Hester Piozzi (1741–1821), who surveyed the territory from the perspective of a rich Englishwoman married to an Italian musician—in her words this made her "demi-naturalized." When first published, her *Observations and Reflections Made in the Course of a Journey through France, Italy and Germany* (1789) was seen as violating a certain type of Grand Tour etiquette. Rather than a classical narrative emphasizing the cultural primacy of ancient Rome, Piozzi offered a stream of personal reflections and observations, not all of them flattering. In fact, her first-hand account gave the typical well-to-do traveler a candid picture of the pains and pleasures arising—often simultaneously—on any visit to the Continent. On descending the Italian side of the Alps she noted "the proportion of terror is just sufficient to mingle with the pleasure and make one feel the full effect of sublimity."

Regarding other scenes, Piozzi was less forgiving. The arches of Turin she found "formed to defend passengers from the rain and sun" but "used for the very grossest of purposes and polluted with smells that poison all one's pleasure." Olfactory concerns were always bubbling to the surface. Rome had a "galaxy of rarities," "which dazzles, diverts, confounds, and nearly fatigues one," but they were housed in places where the "*odori*" were "nasty beyond all telling and all endurance." Elsewhere the problem was that the sun in Italy was just too bright. In Florence, "blindness seem[ed] no uncommon misfortune ... from the strong reverberation of the sun's rays on houses of the cleanest and most brilliant white." Piozzi often compared the sights to those back home, not quite seeing what the fuss was about: "the tower at Bridgnorth in Shropshire leans exactly in the same direction, and is full as much out of the perpendicular as this at Pisa." In Vicenza, she "fatigued" herself "to death almost by walking three miles out of town, to see the famous villa from whence Merriworth Castle in Kent was modelled." Her considered verdict? Palladio's Villa Rotonda was "inferior in everything but situation to Merriworth, and with that patriotic consolation I leave Vicenza."

Despite the stench at St Mark's, Piozzi was seduced by Venice. Arriving in the city after an eight-hour journey by barge with her new husband, she took in a view that up to then she had seen only in Canaletto's paintings: "I do believe that Venice, like other Italian beauties, will be observed to possess features so striking, so prominent, and so discriminated, that her portrait, like theirs, will not be found difficult to take, nor the impression she has once made easy to erase. British charms captivate less powerfully, less certainly, less suddenly ... The general effect produced by such architecture, such painting, such pillars; illuminated as I saw them last night by the moon at full, rising out of the sea, produced an effect like enchantment."

To travel with a consumptive relative

Mariana Starke (1762–1836)—playwright, poet, translator, travel writer, "mistress of Latin, Greek and oriental languages"—published *Letters from Italy* in 1802. Her 25 letters, written over seven years (1792–98), spanned two volumes, forming a kind of proto-Baedeker that offered both fledgling and seasoned tourists an enthusiastically detailed itinerary. Aware of the increasing number of Britons eager to make the trip, *Letters* reached beyond the artistic and architectural descriptions of earlier guidebooks (usually intended for wealthier grand tourists) to instead provide a wider audience with a wealth of useful, budget-friendly advice while abroad. Starke gave tips on where to stay (in Naples, "persons who wish for an air congenial to weak lungs should live in the *Fouria*"); what to do and how to get there ("For a coach and four horses to Pompeii the usual price is eight *ducats* ... to the Boy who carries your dinner to the Villa it is usual to give two *carlini*). For the musically inclined, Starke could advise on the "hire of a Pianoforte," and to all she cautioned, "Travelers should not have their baggage plumbed at Pisa."

As for "things necessary for an invalid to be provided with on leaving England," Starke left no stone unturned. Her two-and-a-half pages of recommendations include: "a cot, to be constructed that it may be transformed into a sofa-bed ... two pillows, two blankets ...napkins (strong, but not fine), pistols, knives ... a traveling *chaise-percée*, made to fit the well of a carriage ... a tea and sugar chest ... curry powder, ketchup, soy, mustard, Cayenne-pepper ... pen-knives, wafers, razors ... cork or common double-soled shoes and boots, which are absolutely needful in order to resist the chill of brick and marble floors ... De la Lande's *Account of Italy*," and "a rhubarb-grater." In addition to practical tips, *Letters from Italy* included Starke's personal "view of the revolutions," of which she concluded: "I am strongly inclined to believe that English Families traveling for health may, at this moment, reside in any City of Italy with as little risk of inconvenience attributable to war, as they could before the invasion of BUONAPARTE." The book became a best-seller.

Starke also had a keen eye for art and used a somewhat manic system of exclamation marks, similar to a star-rating, to chart cultural highs and lows: in Rome one could see "people blowing glass by Gerard della Notte !—a fruit-woman and her child, by Guercino !!—a Claude !!!—... two pictures, by N. Poussin, one representing the Madonna and our Savior with Angels !!!!" (A "Head of Medusa, by Leonardo da Vinci" received just "!!!")

To transport Italianate into the cold light of the north

Bernardo Bellotto (*c* 1721–1780) first painted his neoclassical view of the *Villa Perabò-Melzi at Gazzada* (1743–44) in the evening light, against a backdrop of snowclad Alps. The white villa and informal vernacular of the outer buildings set out a code for the transition from baroque composition to an essentially modern juxtaposing of independent and self-contained forms. A taste for this new mode of cubic volume and unframed windows is also evident in Colen Campbell's *Vitrivius Britannicus* of 1715–25, in the remark, "the whole is dressed very plain ... most conformable to the simplicity of the ancients," or in Schinkel's 1834 Gardener's House in Sanssouci Park in Potsdam, where an ornamental white tabernacle (a tea pavilion) cohabits with the "Roman baths," a more rustic yellow ensemble of juxtaposed geometric volumes.

The combination of reduced functional buildings (usually yellow) with simulated antique temples (white villas) became the nineteenth century's preferred template of forms. As baroque unity and centrality dissolved into receding and advancing masses, scenic arrangements of elementary forms came increasingly to resemble the plain walls and cubic volumes of the Italian vernacular which had, perhaps subliminally, influenced generations of grand tourists. This was a picturesque ambition, a composition of forms that had survived a transalpine migration to zones of cool northern light, now divorced and estranged from the *chiaroscuro* evening atmosphere of Lombardy.

Italianate was also the style of choice for those pioneers of brutalism, Alison and Peter Smithson, whose London office and residence—Cato Lodge—is an essay in nineteenth-century suburban romanticism. Located at the corner of Priory Walk and Gilston Road, South Kensington, its fragmented and juxtaposed volumes combine the white stucco and tripartite arched windows of Italian villas with sturdy cubic volumes in London stock bricks, which are initially yellow, but quickly take on a patina of gray grime—a signature of the city's coal-fired past. Below the Smithsons' tripartite arched windows hover three delicate plaster garland motifs, or swags as they are known in English.

Temple of Hercules at Cori, after Théodore Labrouste, 2014
$2^{11}/_{64} \times 2^{3}/_{4}$" (5.5 × 7 CM)

Peter Smithson addressed the subject of such "attachments" in his *AD* essay "Once a Jolly Swagman," an ode inspired by seeing Théodore Labrouste's 1831 rendering of the Temple of Hercules at Cori, a drawing "so fine it is almost impossible to reproduce," showing a noble ensemble bedecked in fetishistic awnings, garlands,

Italianate, after Bernardo Bellotto
and Karl Friedrich Schinkel + Cato Lodge, 2012
2 × 5²⁹⁄₃₂" (5 × 15 CM)

fronds, and weaponry. Opening with a photograph of the entrance to Cato Lodge swathed in a drooping garland of woven leaves (strangely, the adjacent plaster swag templates are never mentioned), the text goes on to argue that architecture must be explicitly built "in a language which anticipates further layers of meaning added later by others." This was the moment—sanctioned in such texts by the self-designated "second generation" of modernism—that architecture reopened its doors to the possibility of signification. The article then moves to the younger Labrouste brother, Henri, and his masterpiece: the Bibliothèque Sainte-Geneviève (1851). Girdled by a band of 100 stone garlands with the names of France's most celebrated literary figures engraved in the facade, the monolithic stone box constitutes a readable house of reading—a forerunner, perhaps, of the kind of participatory moment that Smithson advocated.

To be tracked down by Schinkel
to buy cheap ultramarine

Wilhelm Hensel (1794–1861) first traveled to Italy in 1823 on a grant awarded by the King of Prussia in recognition of both his talent for painting (friezes in Berlin's Schauspielhaus, built by his friend and patron Karl Friedrich Schinkel) and his air for enlivening parties (with "living pictures" from *Lalla Rookh*, a popular "Oriental" romance, for a celebration at court in 1821). In return for his stipend he was to make a life-sized copy of Raphael's *Transfiguration*, newly returned to the Vatican after a number of years in the Louvre, war booty of Napoleon. Schinkel also suggested that he produce accurate copies of pictures from Herculaneum to be used as teaching aids at the Akademie der Künste in Berlin. After his departure the love interest in this story, Fanny Mendelssohn Bartholdy (sister of the composer Felix), wrote to his traveling companion, the singer Eduard Devrient, asking him to keep Wilhelm away from the corrupting influence of Catholicism.

In Rome Hensel fell in with the Prussian Consul Jakob Salomon Bartholdy, uncle of his future wife and a central figure for the 38 Prussian and Bavarian artists then living in the city—17 of whom Hensel depicted in a composite tableau celebrating the marriage of the Prussian crown prince. By spring the following year Prussia's first Minister of Culture, Karl vom Stein zum Altenstein, had already become anxious that Hensel was neglecting his duty to deliver copies of Italian artworks. Schinkel, in his capacity as overseer of the Prussian Building Commission, was sent to investigate the Arcadian truant. He arrived in Rome on August 24, 1826 and visited Hensel one week later. By October the artist had finished a portrait of Schinkel, which evidently pleased its subject greatly: he noted in his diary that Hensel's work had found its style in Italy. On October 19 Schinkel reported to Berlin that the artist was diligently fulfilling his contract by copying the Raphael—and further that it would be advisable for this copy to be delivered as a line drawing, to avoid any darkening or loss of quality by paint and shadow. Hensel had, he said, more than satisfied his contract in developing as an artist and was a credit to the Fatherland.

Wilhelm Hensel in the Campagna,
after Maksymiljan Antoni Piotrowski, 2012
$3\,^{15}\!/_{16} \times 3$" (10 × 7.5 CM)

Unfortunately, Hensel's four years in Rome were overshadowed by debt and pressure to deliver work. Overseen from Berlin by his future father-in-law, Abraham Mendelssohn Bartholdy, and tyrannized by the procedural correctness of Prussian administration, Hensel was at one point forced to abandon official commissions and paint commercially to fend off starvation. Towards the end of his stay, he asked Bartholdy for a further 150 louis d'or to purchase ultramarine, which was much cheaper in Italy and most likely used for an altar painting for Potsdam—a commission from Altenstein which helped resolve Hensel's Roman debts.

Before leaving Rome Hensel completed two large-format pictures: the original commission—a copy of Raphael's *Transfiguration*—and the Potsdam altarpiece *Christ and the Samaritan Woman by the Well*. He painted both simultaneously in the Vatican (a solution to the difficulty of finding an adequate studio). Back in Berlin it was noted that Hensel "appears somewhat Catholic."

In 1829 Hensel finally married Fanny. The newlyweds planned to travel to Italy, but life in the extended Mendelssohn Bartholdy family was so filled with engagements, concerts and portrait commissions that it was not until 1839 that they finally set off, accompanied by their nine-year-old son Sebastian. In Rome they mingled with society, diplomatic circles and other German artists. Uncle Solomon's Casa Bartholdy was now occupied by the English and stuffed full of sofas and furniture, a contrast to the ordered collection of frescos Hensel remembered. After deciding to extend their stay, Fanny noted in her diary "it is a great struggle to leave Rome ... I did not expect to be so deeply affected by the atmosphere here," and on the day of their departure: "my poor Wilhelm is in such a mortal and physical state, huge tears in his eyes and unable to speak a word."

To explore a 250m² apartment that wants to be a museum

A very good reason to travel to Italy would be to view an apartment designed by Carlo Scarpa, which only recently came on the market in its original condition. For 25 years the residence, occupied by Scarpa's lawyer friend, was inaccessible. Now the cocoon has been shed and the chrysalis of the house can be explored, its details caressed (black plaster ceiling, samba stair, and door joinery to die for), and its intense and intimate atmosphere (glare screening shutters) experienced at firsthand. Such a spatial survey was enacted by the naked woman artist who exhibited a film of herself dancing through the house at the 2015 Venice Art Biennale. The apartment is now available for an initiated patron (hopefully also a Donna Leon fan) in search of a cultural profile, with €2 million to spare.

Carlo Scarpa, apartment in the Palazzo Michiel, Venice, 2013
3½ × 4 ¹¹⁄₁₆" (9 × 12 CM)

To enjoy the unimpeded view

Catel "wanted to portray me in a little painting that represents a room in Naples, from which one sees through an open window the sea and the island of Capri and the trees of the Villa Reale beneath the window, just the way that I had lived there," Karl Friedrich Schinkel (1781–1841) wrote in his diary on October 23, 1824. The Prussian architect duly appears in Franz Ludwig Catel's painting seated at an open balcony that looks out on a view identical to the one he describes. Counterbalancing his figure on the left are three antique pieces: a fine Panathenaic amphora and a Greek bronze bowl, both from the collection of the Prussian consul in Rome, and a tall bronze candelabrum. But Schinkel did not visit Naples during his 1824 trip. Catel had based his *View of Naples through a Window* on a suite at the Albergo alla Grand Europa that he and Schinkel had rented some years earlier.

For architects a closer look reveals a subliminal liberation from the over-regulated north, where building codes inherited from stringent Prussians (whom Schinkel served) required similarly high windows to have a handrail. This unencumbered view of Capri dissolves any barrier between inside and outside, thus prefiguring one of modernism's principal spatial paradigms.

Schinkel commissioned the painting as a present for his wife back in Berlin, and Catel assembled the composition in his Rome studio. As was often the case with the Grand Tour market, prospective purchasers could specify the people and the signifying artifacts that were to appear in the scene. Writing from Florence on October 28, Schinkel told his wife: "It is intended as your Christmas gift, but unfortunately it will not arrive in time. So instead you will have to content yourself with me alone this Christmas."

Karl Friedrich Schinkel in Naples, after Franz Ludwig Catel, 2014

$7^{3}/_{32} \times 9^{29}/_{64}$" (18 × 24 CM)

To deny Pope Julius II entry into heaven

Desiderius Erasmus of Rotterdam (*c* 1467–1536) arrived in Rome in March 1509. Celebrated for his mastery of Latin and ancient Greek and for his *Adagia*, a recently published collection of ancient proverbs, the leading humanist was given access to the Vatican Library, at that time besieged by the building works initiated by Pope Julius II—the rebuilding of St Peter's by Bramante, the reorganization of the Vatican Palace, the construction of the Belvedere villa and the creation of a new garden for ancient statues (including the newly excavated *Laocoön*). Elsewhere in the city the Via Giulia and various church building projects were underway. But Erasmus was troubled less by these disruptions than by Julius II's belligerent militarism. The comparison he drew was with another Julius—Caesar—also known for his regular and enthusiastic war-making. Others called Julius the Fearsome Pope.

Erasmus left Rome in July 1509. In Cambridge in 1513—from the safety granted by geographical distance, anonymity and the Pope's recent earthly demise—he penned a dialogue, Th*e Sileni of Alcibiades*, in which Julius turns up at the gates of heaven in the same bejeweled tiara and pompous regalia Erasmus had seen him wear on entering a conquered Bologna. St Peter grills him on his corruption, drinking, murders, and syphilis contracted from traffic with courtesans. For these sins and his lack of repentance the spiritual leader of Christendom is, in Erasmus's text, denied entry to paradise.

To pick up the trail of a Leviathan

In 1614 Thomas Hobbes (1588–1679) journeyed to Rome as companion to William Cavendish, son of the first Earl of Devonshire (an early incidence of the preferred tutor + young nobleman template for the Grand Tours undertaken by later generations). Like many travelers of the time Hobbes described Rome as situated in a desert, a particularly unfruitful landscape. After seeing the usual sights, he closely observed papal political structures, which from his Protestant viewpoint were feudal and military. Hobbes' sojourn in Italy also appears to have exposed him to the ideas of Paolo Sarpi, who argued for the supremacy of temporal rulers over religious authorities—a theory that would be indelibly inscribed in his own political philosophy.

In 1620, in a kind of warming up exercise for *Leviathan*, Hobbes anonymously published a text condemning papal nepotism, particularly as it applied to the current pontiff, Paul V (born Camillo Borghese), who had created a special post, "Cardinal Nephew," for Scipione Caffarelli, his sister's son, and showered him with honors and cash-generating ecclesiastical positions—superintendent general of the Papal States, archpriest of the Lateran and Vatican basilicas, Grand Penitentiary, secretary of the Apostolic Briefs, protector of the Shrine of Loreto, etc., etc. A similar largesse was extended to a second nephew, Marcantonio Borghese, when he got old enough. By 1620 more than 600,000 scudi had passed from church coffers into Borghese hands, financing along the way the construction of the grandiose Villa Borghese, with its extensive gardens and art collection. Hobbes concluded that the Church preached poverty but practiced luxurious wealth.

In Part III of his *Horae Subsecivae: Observations and Discourses*, Hobbes advised English Protestants to travel to Rome incognito. The city, he wrote, was infested with a network of exiled English Catholic spies, who would gladly denounce them to the Inquisition for torture and conversion by force. Italians were also not to be trusted, especially not physicians, who were obliged to inform the Inquisition of any failure on their patient's part to take confession or communion when gravely ill.

To be celebrated as a child prodigy

After Angelika Kauffmann's self-portrait, aged 12, 2013
1⅜ × 1³⁄₁₆" (3.5 × 3 CM)

Born in Chur, Switzerland, Angelika Kauffmann (1741–1807) learned from an early age to capitalize on her parallel aptitudes for music and painting, encouraged all the way by her business-minded father, the itinerant late-baroque portraitist and fresco painter Johan Joseph Kauffmann (1707–1782). A self-portrait of Angelika at 12—dressed in the bucolic shepherdess style then favored by the aristocracy, and holding the score for a canon by the fashionable poet and librettist Pietro Metastasio—projects an aspirational, civilized life of music and poetry.

That same year the family relocated to Como, then part of the Austrian Empire and a city made wealthy by silk production. The young Angelika immediately got to work, drawing a pastel portrait of the Bishop Monsignor Neuroni. Three years later, the *Wunderkind* charmed Francis III of Este, Duke of Modena, with a portrait of his son Ercole. The Duke allowed Angelika to study his collection of old masters and further commissions followed. Angelika's rigorous training by Kauffmann Sr, paired with her innate skills not only as a painter but as a singer and polyglot, furnished her with the refined manners that enabled her to move easily in the upper echelons of European society. After the death of her mother Cleophea in 1757, father and daughter could be found in Schwarzenberg, Vorarlberg, painting church frescos. A self-portrait by Angelika from this time, dressed now in local vernacular costume, has hung in the Uffizi in Florence since 1772.

After Angelika Kauffmann's self-portraits,
aged 16 and 24 (in the manner of Raphael), 2012
Both 1⅜ × 1³⁄₁₆" (3.5 × 3 CM)

To become an academician

Angelika Kauffmann's ascent in a male-dominated world can be charted by her election, while she was still in her twenties, to the Academies in Bologna and Florence (1762), Rome (1765) and London (1768). Dubbed the "female Raphael" (coincidentally, the painting she presented to the Roman Academy was a self-portrait done in his style), Kauffmann made full use of her new accolades, painting flattering portraits of the tourists in Italy who could best promote her, from the Shakespearean actor and theater producer David Garrick (1707–1779) to the father of art history, Johann Joachim Winckelmann. While her figures were criticized for their inaccurate anatomy—as a woman she was banned from life-classes with male models—her later works often depicted Greek heroines, such as Ariadne and Calypso, Penelope at her loom or the three goddesses Athena, Aphrodite and Hera. English travelers versed in Ovid, Virgil, and Homer became the principal clients for Kauffmann's paintings of classical mythology. Always the career strategist, in 1766 she moved to London, where the Danish ambassador reported "the whole world is angelica mad." Her greatest champion, Sir Joshua Reynolds, called her "Miss Angel." A 1775 self-portrait as a grand London lady hangs in the National Portrait Gallery.

After Angelika Kauffmann's self-portraits, aged 34 and 40, 2012
Both 1⅜ × 1³⁄₁₆" (3.5 × 3 CM)

To make a lot of money and see it dwindle away

London loved Angelika Kauffmann. Here, she enjoyed unprecedented financial success: her paintings of classical goddesses were converted into mass-produced copper plate reproductions, while Wedgwood and Derby churned out porcelain serializations of her fashionably sentimental allegorical motifs. It was in London, too, that Kauffmann met her first husband, a fine-looking man who lived at Claridge's and claimed to be—but wasn't—a Count Frederick de Horn. The "Count's" death in 1780 freed her to marry again; this time she chose the Venetian painter Antonio Zucchi. After 15 years in London, the time seemed ripe for a return to Italy, particularly in the wake of anti-Catholic riots instigated by Lord George Gordon. The couple and their entourage went first to Venice, where the Russian Crown Prince, Pavel Petrovich, purchased three of Kauffmann's paintings. In Naples the following June she met Maria Carolina—daughter of the Austrian Empress, sister of Marie Antoinette and the wife of Ferdinand IV, the Bourbon King of Naples. After painting the royal couple, their six children and three dogs, Kauffmann was invited to join the court as the official painter. She turned down the offer, preferring to set up a studio of her own in Rome, where she took over a house in Via Sistina once occupied by the German painter Anton Raphael Mengs.

Kauffmann's studio and salon soon became a flytrap for tourists visiting from England, Germany, Russia, and Poland. A self-portrait from around this time, now hanging in the Neue Pinakothek in Munich, shows a youthful 43-year-old "charmer of all Europe" wearing neoclassical finery. Goethe was one of those who made his way to the salon, right after his arrival in Rome in 1786. The two became friends, and she painted his portrait—he is shown as sensitive, vulnerable, almost feminine, perhaps too revealing a psychogram for her subject, who declared "he's a handsome enough chap, but not a bit of me in him." Kauffmann and her clique's monopolizing of the tourist trade naturally caused some resentment among other artists in Rome. Unabashedly business-like, she had her price list hanging on the wall of her studio:

Subject with life-size figure—120 zecchini for each figure
Two secondary figures count as one principal figure and cost the same
For the background of the picture the cost is the same as for a principal figure
Historic subjects with figures in half life-size—60 zecchini for each principal figure
A portrait of a head, without hands—40 zecchini
Half the price is to be paid at the first sitting

This idyll came to an end with the death of her husband in 1795 and the advance of Napoleon into Italy the following year, which disrupted Kauffmann's trade with the courts of Europe. In the last years of her life the artist found herself out of fashion: "the poverty does not terrify me, but the loneliness kills me," she confided to a friend. But her fellow academicians did not forget her. When Kauffmann died in 1807, a funeral procession comprising the entire Accademia di San Luca followed her body to her tomb in Sant'Andrea delle Fratte.

To find a way out

"I only discovered my talent when my first drawing was published in Milan. It took me ten minutes to do, but when it appeared in the paper, I looked at it for hours and was mesmerized." For Saul Steinberg this first drawing, on page 3 of the October 27, 1936 issue of the satirical paper *Bertoldo*, marked the beginning of "paradise." He was three years into a seven-year sojourn in Italy, having abandoned the "cesspool" of anti-Semitic Bucharest in 1933 to study architecture in Milan. Until this point he had been a cash-strapped student at the Politecnico, taking refuge in a series of *pensiones* and "gigantic portions of *rigatoni al sugo* ... followed by goulash or stew drowned in red sauce, which you mopped up with the endless bread." Suddenly with his *Bertoldo* breakthrough, the future looked bright. He "could make a living ... eat and sleep, buy neckties." He stopped going to class and spent the next two years producing cartoons for the magazine and its supplement *Arcibertoldo*. But even in paradise, even when working under a pseudonym, Steinberg could not escape the wave of anti-Semitism that was gaining ground in Fascist Italy. All publications had to adhere to tight guidelines, and even satirical reviews were forced to bow to political pressure—the same magazine that published Steinberg's very first cartoon also carried, on the front page of the same issue, a reproduction of a telegram declaring "44 MILLION ITALIANS EXPRESS THEIR GRATITUDE"

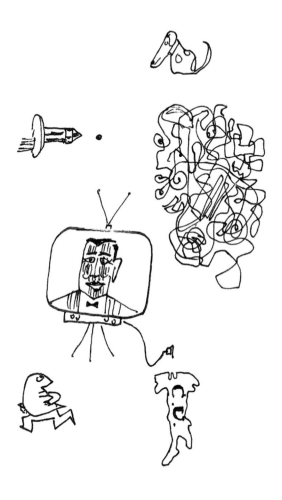

CU in Italy, after Saul Steinberg, 2013

$3\,^{15}\!/_{16} \times 2\,^{23}\!/_{64}$" (10 × 6 CM)

to Mussolini on the anniversary of the founding of the Fascist party. By the summer of 1938, under new race laws, Steinberg—or more precisely, "Steinberg Saul of Moritz, Romanian Jew," as he was listed in Italian police records—had to leave his job. He was almost forced to abandon architecture school too, but was granted one year to catch up—12 months into which to cram 16 exams originally scheduled over five years of study—and to secure a way out of the country where "stupid society [was] turning against" him. For his graduation project, delivered on what seems to have been the last possible day for submissions, he presented a design for a theater. No evidence of such a project remains, but according to *Bertoldo*'s co-editor Vittorio Metz, at the theater entrance Steinberg drew a stick-person holding a lance and straddling a cow "to indicate the proportions."

After graduating, Steinberg spent the rest of the year and all of 1940 trying to escape the worsening situation in Italy. With the help of the American publisher Cesare Civita he obtained a Dominican visa and a ticket for passage to New York via Lisbon. However, when his flight from Barcelona landed at Lisbon airport, Steinberg was denied entry and forced to go back. Reluctantly returning to Milan, he raced to get his paperwork in order while trying to remain undetected by the authorities. He laid low in his apartment above the Bar del Grillo, stayed in the houses and studios of colleagues like Aldo Buzzi, and even found time to have an affair and make trips to the cinema. In February 1941 a warrant was issued for his arrest and internment on the grounds that his passport and transit visas had expired. On April 27, 1941 he turned himself in at San Vittore prison (writing in his journal, "downstairs at 9. Shave. In a taxi with two policemen. Telephone Adina. She already knows, dear girl, she was at Ferraro's. Station, Buzzi with the suitcases"). Three days later he arrived at the Tortoreto internment camp in Teramo, where he soon became known as the "romantic young man who fascinated all the girls on account of his good looks." Even here he continued to draw and paint. Just over a month after his arrest, with the help of the Delegation for the Assistance of Jewish Emigrants, Steinberg was released in order to make a flight from Rome to Lisbon. From there he boarded the SS *Excalibur* to New York and then traveled on to Santo Domingo, where he finally secured an American visa.

"Tomorrow is New Year's Day," Steinberg had written in his diary on December 31, 1940. "I hope to be able to go on to see in 42 whether 41 has been good or bad for me." It would not turn out to be a good year—he reflected some 50 years later—but "how lucky I was to be saved." "I took a night train from Rome, seated, with all the perils, police, documents. Arrived safely in Milan ... At night I returned to Rome, a crowded train, nameless hotel, on Via dei Chiavari, I think, in the Ghetto. Saved from minute to minute by a miracle. The only thing remaining in my mind is the beautiful maid in the hotel, going up and down the narrow staircase."

Steinberg would return to Milan in 1954—now as an American citizen, having already made a name for himself as an illustrator—to work with Ernesto Rogers (also a graduate of the Politecnico) and BBPR studio on the design of the Children's Labyrinth at the Milan X Triennale. He was responsible for producing the free-hand line drawings that were enlarged and applied using sgraffito across its long walls.

In 1971, thirty years after his flight from Italy, he produced a series of drawings of remembrances from Milan for the *New Yorker*. At first these memory postcards seem to objectively capture glimpses of the city in the architectural style of the time. A closer look reveals a more cynical view: blank soldiers march and men salute each other against what Steinberg coined the "Milanese Bauhaus," where stacked apartments, sweeping art deco facades, and white churches with curved corners serve not only as the backdrop for Mussolini's regime, but as a complete manifestation of paradise lost.

To compensate for certain
shortcomings at home

Werner Oechslin's weighty 2008 gta/ETH Zurich tome on European and American Palladianism concludes that, in England at least, the style was a compensation for inherent national shortcomings. Already in 1731 Alexander Pope had admonished Lord Burlington:

You show us, Rome was glorious, not profuse,
and pompous buildings once were things of use.
Yet shall (my Lord) your just, your noble rules
Fill half the land with imitating fools;
Who random drawings from your sheets shall take,
And of one beauty many blunders make...
Or call the winds through long arcades to roar,
Proud to catch cold at a Venetian door;
Conscious they act a true Palladian part,
And, if they starve, they starve by rules of art.

But nothing changed. Forty years on, Horace Walpole still felt obliged to observe that "mere mechanic knowledge may avoid faults, without furnishing beauties," or that "grace does not depend on rules" and "taste is not to be learnt."

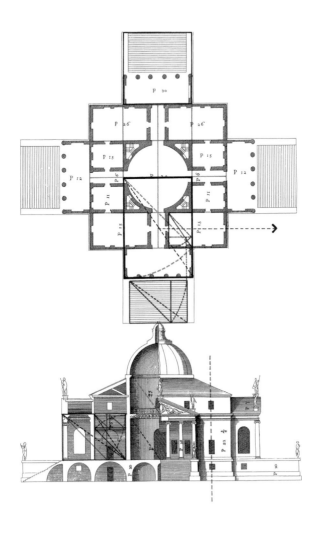

Andrea Palladio, La Rotunda, golden section analysis, 2012
5½ × 4²¹⁄₆₄" (14 × 11 CM)

To play a good stick
upon the violoncello

The artist Alexander Cozens (1717–1786), born in Russia to British parents, set sail from St Petersburg in 1746 on the first leg of a two-year tour of Italy. Nearly all of the drawings he produced on this visit were lost after they reportedly fell out of his saddlebag. The well-connected Cozens—his godfather was Tsar Peter I—enjoyed considerable success as a landscape painter. His pupils included the Prince of Wales, and he was the drawing master at Christ's Hospital and, later, Eton College. He also developed the "blot" technique for making landscapes. His 1785 treatise, *A New Method of Assisting the Invention in Drawing Original Compositions of Landscape*, describes how to make more imaginative landscapes by co-opting the suggestive compositional potential of accidental ink stains on a piece of paper. The results—claimed his friend, the wealthy William Beckford—were "almost as full of systems as the universe."

After John Robert Cozens, Castel Gandolfo and Lake Albano, 2022
3¹¹⁄₃₂ × 4⁵⁹⁄₆₄" (8.5 × 12.5 CM)

One of Cozens' most loyal followers was his son, John Robert Cozens (1752–1797), who arrived in Italy in August 1776 in the company of the classical scholar Richard Payne Knight. In Florence Cozens Jr found—and purchased—a large cache of the drawings his father had lost 30 years before. While his name afforded him enough commissions to earn a living, he kept his work out of the public eye. His silent, hesitating disposition is evident in the subtle watercolors he produced in the Roman Campagna—a departure from his father's style in their use of muted tones. "Little Cozens," as his friend Thomas Jones called him, was also commissioned by Payne Knight to make watercolors of Sicily from sketches by Charles Gore and Philipp Hackert. After briefly returning to England, John Robert was back in Italy in 1782, painting landscapes for his father's friend, the extravagant and demanding Beckford. The relationship was strained. After contracting malaria Cozens went to stay with Sir William Hamilton while Beckford toured the country. "The vermin plays a good stick upon the violoncello, which was a fine discovery," wrote Hamilton to Beckford. "We played 4 hours. He has made some charming sketches, but I see by his book that he is indolent as usual." Not everyone agreed—John Constable called him "the greatest genius that ever touched landscape."

To become "farre lesse pufft up'

As a German, a scholar and a long-term resident in Rome, Johann Joachim Winckelmann (1717–1768) was of the opinion that "the lethargic temperament of the English, coupled with the unfortunate climate in which they had to live, was bound to inhibit the development of their aesthetic sense." To remedy this intolerable deficiency, then, it was essential for Englishmen to undertake a tour in Italy, preferably under the guidance of a *cicerone* of Winckelmann's stature.

A century earlier, in the years of the English Civil War, the covert Catholic agitator Richard Lassels (1603–1668) had been the best informed bear-leader for young Catholics in voluntary exile. He wrote that "he who hath seen so many men and greater estates than his own comes home far more modest and civil … farre lesse pufft up." His *Voyage of Italy, or a Compleat Journey Through Italy: in Two Parts*—"the best directions for European travel," according to his contemporary, John Aubrey—was published in Paris in 1670. For the second 1698 edition printed in London, contentious pro-Catholic comments were excised, so new readers never got to know, for example, about a marble plaque in the Basilica of Sant'Andrea in Padua commemorating the burial of the bowels of Thomas Howard, Earl of Arundel (*"Interiora Thomae Howardi Comitis Arondelae"*). Lassels interpreted this interment of vital organs as a sign of Howard's ultimate commitment to Rome. Although he had officially converted to Anglicanism in December 1616, on becoming a member of the Privy Council, Howard was also known as the leader of English Catholics. After dying in Padua his body was speedily returned to England for an Anglican burial—playing both sides of the fence in death as he had done in life, with Italy providing the preferred intellectual and aesthetic platform.

To find a hell that is really heaven

John Milton (1608–1674) may well have based his description of Tartarus in *Paradise Lost* (1667) on the smoldering Solfatara caldera, which he would have seen in 1638 on his way to Naples, where the women, he noted, were "generally well featur'd, but excessively libidinous." If so, he was only following in the footsteps of Virgil (70–19BC), who had Aeneas descend into the underworld from Lake Avernus, which fills the crater of an extinct volcano in nearby Pozzuoli. Recent scientific research has concluded that the Devil's stink of sulfurous steam rising from the bubbling mud pits of the restive caldera is in fact a natural Viagra (a cocktail of H_2S, N_2O, H_2O, CH_4, He, C_9): hydrogen sulphide, H_2S, instigates men's erections.

Those seeking longer, more enduring exposure are encouraged to camp in the steamy crater.

Milton's evocative equation of Paradise with the sylvan Paradisino above Vallombrosa would inspire many of the Romantic generation, among them Wordsworth, Trollope, and Mary Shelley, to beat the same path to the remote Tuscan monastery. Whether Milton actually set foot in Vallombrosa, or saw for himself the Etrurian shades overlooking the valley of the Arno, is today hotly debated. Regardless of the academic controversy, a fascist-era plaque on the Paradisino wall testifies to Milton's influential, and possibly fictitious, visit.

To buy 300 pictures

George Johnstone, 3rd Marquess of Annandale (1720–1792), is reported to have returned to Scotland in 1738 with 300 pictures—although this avid consumer of art may in fact have been his father William Johnstone, 1st Marquess of Annandale (1663–1721), who returned from Italy in 1713 with "bookes and pictures." The 3rd Marquess traveled to Italy at the age of 17 and was complimented in Siena for his exemplary behavior, befitting a Scottish gentleman. His traveling companion, George Sinclair of Ulbster, subsequently related that Annandale had "f...ed a girl on Ponte St Angelo" after getting "d...k." Annandale was reported by friends to have gone insane sometime between 1743–48, although not before changing his name to Van den Bempde in order to inherit a fortune from a relative on his mother's side.

Not to bathe

When Napoleon was crowned King of Italy in 1805 he made his sister, Elisa Bonaparte Baciocchi, Grand Duchess of Tuscany. The granduchessa undertook some modifications to the Palazzo Pitti, Tuscan seat of the short-lived Franco-Italian empire, in the hope of enticing her brother to visit—a bathroom designed by the architect Giuseppe Cacialli, with lunettes and statues of Venus bathing by Salvatore Bongiovanni, taps with winged figures by Marco Corsini, and spindly side tables in petrified wood, all in the latest neoclassical style. Unfortunately her brother never made it to Italy to disrobe in this exquisite tableau, which still bears his name, so that passing tourists today invariably comment on the smallness of the marble tub and make deductions on the emperor's stature.

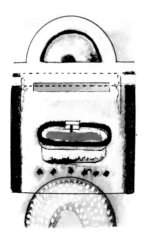

Napoleon's unused bath, 2022
3 5/32 × 5 3/32" (8 × 13 CM)

To attend a gathering of the International Imaginist Bauhaus

Casa Asger Jorn, Albisola, 2022
$3\frac{5}{32} \times 4\frac{11}{16}$" (8 × 12 CM)

In 1954 the Danish artist Asger Jorn moved to Albisola, where he took over two ancient Ligurian houses and made them into a "total work of art," complete with sculptures, ceramics (the town's specialty), and large murals. He also found time to organize a gathering of artists, bringing together old friends from his Cobra days, such as Constant Nieuwenhuys and Christian Dotremont, and newer local acquaintances like a young Ettore Sottsass and the painter/pharmacist mayor of nearby Alba, Giuseppe Gallizio. This "experimental laboratory for free artistic research" proclaimed its opposition to the orthodoxy of Gropius: "The leaders of the old Bauhaus were great masters with exceptional talents," Jorn said, "but they were poor teachers. The students' works were only pious imitations of their masters ... This is not at all a criticism, it is simply a recognition of reality ... the direct transfer of artistic gifts is impossible." A banquet sponsored by the "important" local chocolatier Ferrero rounded off the event.

In *Exit Utopia* Sottsass wrote that "when we arrived at the entrance to the firm's vast reception hall Mr Ferrero, our sponsor ... received us dressed in black with a black necktie—just as one should present oneself at an international convention. There were only 15 of us; somewhat despairing and perplexed Mr Ferrero asked: "Are you all here?" "Yes," we said, "We're all here." Mr Ferrero opened the door of the great hall and there in front of us—perfectly laid out and decked with flowers for a group of at least 40 people—was a table more than 20m long. We all hovered there, speechless and a bit embarrassed."

"Anyway," Sottsass reflected, "the symposium went very well, and we were all very pleased."

To be barbecued

Percy Bysshe Shelley, 2012
2 × 1³⁷⁄₆₄" (5 × 4 CM)

Percy Bysshe Shelley drowned in July 1822. A sudden storm in the Gulf of Spezia was to blame, though Mary Shelley talked of the unseaworthiness of his open sailing boat, the *Don Juan*, specially constructed for him in Genoa, and there were also rumors of piracy or even political assassination (Shelley had become an enemy of the British establishment when he penned "The Necessity of Atheism"). Due to Italian quarantine laws, his sea-mutilated body could not be transported to Rome to be buried near the Pyramid of Cestius, alongside his friend and fellow-poet John Keats. As the next best thing, his fellow visionary Romantics planned a mock-Hellenic cremation on the beach near Viareggio, where his remains had washed up. The ceremony was to be an enactment of Keats' words from *Ode to a Nightingale*, to "take into the air my quiet breath"—the "Romantic desire for assimilation into the air ... desired to assume illimitability," as Steven Connor put it in T*he Matter of Air: Science and the Art of the Ethereal*. Edward John Trelawny was charged with the cremation but, as he later reported, the fire got somewhat out of hand. When the corpse fell open, laying bare the heart, and brains bubbled on steel bars, the Romantics retreated—Leigh Hunt to cower behind the closed windows of his carriage, Byron for a swim.

To garden / Ad hortum

One reason to travel to Italy would be to visit the Hortus Urbis Garden in Rome, stocked only with plants named by Latin authors (Columella, Pliny the Elder, Cato, Virgil) and used by ancient Romans. Located within the Parco Regionale dell'Appia Antica (which itself preserves a fragment of the ancient Roman countryside and a number of archaeological ruins), the garden is part of the *Zappata romana* initiative—a collective action for the appropriation of urban public space (vacant or abandoned sites) and the development of environmental, economic, and social issues. The project began in 2010 with a survey of existing community gardens which were uploaded to Google Maps. By 2013 more than 100 spontaneous or shared gardens had been added to zappataromana.net. Such productions represent what Saskia Sassen has termed "new forms of citizenship." These rhetorical and operational openings—space-making through bottom-up actions—circumvent the traditional top-down rituals of consumerism. Today the Hortus Urbis, located in the footprint of a former paper mill, offers two-hour cooking lessons on Saturday mornings which allow for a sampling of the plants. Themes include *pizzoccheri* and flavored/colored pasta (*maltagiati* with sage, *paglia e fieno*).

To publish "Italy as it really is—
a warning for all who intend to travel there'

The lawyer and Prussian official Gustav Alexander Wilhelm Nicolai (1795–1850) attempted to burst the Italy bubble. His 1833 publication, *Italien wie es wirklich ist*, described filthy accommodation, mean landscapes, bandits, and devilish venereal disease—terror in the lemon groves. Although heavily criticized, in particular by Friedrich Wilhelm Gubitz, it won its author an Arts and Sciences Gold Medal from Kaiser Friedrich Wilhelm III, who had contributed to the book's introduction.

While Nicolai took his lead from Heinrich Heine's description of Italy as "a land of sunburn and fleas," criticism was not an approved activity in Prussia. The "put-down" was ignored and the terrain of Italy maintained its mythical aura well into the Romantic and modern eras.

To paint a wall

Thomas Jones (1742–1803), a landscape painter and dedicated pupil of fellow Welshman Richard Wilson, was in Italy from 1776 to 1783. His autobiography, *Memoirs of Thomas Jones of Penkerrig*, offers insightful and detailed descriptions of the painters and life he found there. On arriving in Rome, Jones met many of his compatriots at the English Coffee House, which he described as "a filthy vaulted room, the walls of which were painted with Sphinxes, Obelisks, and Pyramids, from capricious designs by Piranesi, and fitter to adorn the inside of an Egyptian Sepulcher than a room of social convention."

In Rome, changing lodgings became his habit, his grounds for this nomadic behavior including: a melancholy chamber hung with dirty and dismal pictures—an unscrupulous landlady—an overexcitable Italian co-resident—his freshly painted pictures being coated with dust stirred up by the antics of a Sicilian adventurer on the floor above. In 1779 he moved into rooms vacated by the watercolorist

William Pars; his new upstairs neighbor was the ageing painter Anton Raphael Mengs, whose work, he noted, was the result of "German phlegmatic Industry." Despite his domestic turmoil Jones discovered the Roman Campagna, in particular the area around Lake Nemi, which, as a faithful Wilsonite, he described as "beautiful and picturesque." Together with John Robert Cozens he made studies in oil of the scenery surrounding a villa outside the Porta Pia. His first commission in Rome was a sunset view of Lake Albano for Frederick Augustus Hervey, the eccentric Earl Bishop of Derry.

Frederick Augustus Hervey, Earl Bishop of Derry, 2012
1⅜ × 1⅜" (3.5 × 3.5 CM)

In 1780 Jones eloped with a Danish widow to Naples, where he found spacious apartments with studio and showroom on the Dogana del Sale, though the noise, filth, and confusion of the quayside soon set him apartment-hopping again. He befriended the watercolorist Don Tito Lusieri, who introduced him to Angelika Kauffmann. Hackert visited his studio and finally Sir William Hamilton began to notice him, instigating another move to the court end of town. In August 1783 he returned to England after receiving an inheritance from his father: he took with him his paramour, their two daughters and a cylinder containing all his paintings—removed from their straining frames and rolled.

While Jones painted landscapes that dutifully conformed to eighteenth-century allegorical convention (*Mount Vesuvius from Torre dell'Annunziata near Naples*, 1783), he was also one of the first to paint outdoors, in the Bay of Naples in 1782. He produced for himself a series of remarkable studies in oil on paper: close-ups of Neapolitan walls and skylines that are carefully composed and rendered in elevation—an abstraction that in recent years has led Jones to be reassessed as an important predecessor of both *plein air* direct observation (nineteenth-century impressionist mode) and abstract composition. This radical formatting—Italy as experienced—eclipses the tropes of antique idealization to engender a new compositional regime. The art historian Svetlana Alpers identifies a conundrum in these tiny, immediately experienced expanses of outdoor space. In paintings like *A Wall in Naples* (11.4 × 16 CM)—now hanging in Room 42 of London's National Gallery—she reads the close handling and frozen light of a still-life, a fragment of the cityscape rendered as an object and transferred to the tabletop indoors, back in the studio.

To be intimidated by a wall in Naples

"...that blue limpid sky, above the roofs, above the ruins of the houses, above the green trees whose boughs were thick with birds. It was that lofty canopy of raw silk, that cold, brilliant blue sky, into which the sea infused a vague nebulous green luminosity: that soft heartless sky which seemed pink and tender as the skin of a child where it hung in a gentle curve over the hill of Posicipo.

"But the point at which that sky looked softest and most heartless was directly above the wall... The wall that forms the background to the courtyard of the Cappella Vecchia is high and sheer. Its plaster is all cracked with age and through exposure to the elements, though once no doubt it was of the same red color as the houses of Herculaneum and Pompeii, the color which Neapolitan painters call Rosso Borbonico.

"Time, sun, rain and neglect had faded and softened that vivid red, giving it the color of flesh, pink here, pale there and, farther off, transparent as a hand before a flame of a candle, and whether on account of the cracks or the green patches visible in patches of mold, or the white, ivory and yellow tints which were visible in places on the ancient plaster, or the play of light whose constant variations were *due to its reflecting the continual irregular movement of the sea, or the restless vagaries of the wind, which modifies the color of light accordingly as it blows from the mountain or from the water—whatever the reason it seemed to me that the high and ancient wall had life, that it was a living thing, a wall of flesh, in which all the experiences to which human flesh is subject were represented, from the pink innocence of babyhood to the green and yellow melancholy of life's decline.*

"It seemed to me that that wall of flesh was gradually withering; and on its surface could be seen those white, green, ivory and pale yellow tints which characterize human flesh when it is weary, old, scored with wrinkles, and ready for the final marvelous experience of dissolution. Big flies wandered slowly over that wall of flesh, humming. The ripe fruit of the day was turning soft and decaying, the sky, that cruel Neapolitan sky, so pure and tender, was filling the weary air over which the first shades of evening had already cast their blight, with misgiving, with regret, and a sad and fleeting happiness. Suddenly a window opened in that wall and a voice called me by name…"

Curzio Malaparte, *The Skin*, 1949

Wall in Naples, 2015
4 $^{59}/_{64}$ × 4 $^{21}/_{64}$" (12.5 × 11 CM)

To see

"Virginia is a good start for Italy." This was the sentiment Cy Twombly's mother voiced in 1952 as the Lexington-born artist prepared for an eight-month sojourn in Europe and North Africa. With a traveling scholarship from the Richmond Museum of Fine Arts, and accompanied by his friend Robert Rauschenberg, Twombly made his way through Rome, Florence, Siena, Assisi, and Venice, continuing to Morocco, Casablanca, Marrakesh, the Atlas Mountains, Tangier, and Tetuan, and back again to Rome. At the Palazzo dei Conservatori Rauschenberg photographed his companion, standing tall, slender, and upright, awed by and contemplating the gigantic and imperiously gesturing stone hand of the Colossus of Constantine. This tête-à-tête between the young traveler and antiquity, the photograph captures Twombly's entire approach to painting, his desire to reinvigorate the aesthetic language of abstract expressionism with the myths of the Mediterranean. On the same contact sheet as Constantine's pointed finger Rauschenberg included six shots of Twombly on the steps of the Basilica di Santa Maria in Aracoeli—five of these would make up *Cy + Roman Steps (I–V)*. Each photograph closes in on the artist until his torso fills the frame, juxtaposing the denim-clad southern boy against the endless, sunlit stone stairs behind him. Virginia may have been a good start for Italy, but Italy marked a major turning point in Cy's life.

Twombly left New York for Italy again in 1957. Some saw his relocation as a rejection of the role that had been ascribed to him as Pollock's successor, but "actually, it wasn't all that scholarly, my reason for going to Rome," he reflected in a 2000 interview with David Sylvester. "I liked the life." He spent that first summer in a house on the Isle of Procida and the autumn in Rome, where he rented an apartment looking out on the Colosseum and painting *Olympia*, *Sunset*, *Blue Room*, and *Arcadia*. He held his first solo show at the Galleria La Tartaruga before going back to America the following

Landscape Transfixed by a Roman Road/Piazza,
after Twombly, after Poussin, 2013
4 ^{59}/$_{64}$ × 6 ^{11}/$_{16}$" (12.5 × 17 CM)

year and marrying the Italian Tatiana Franchetti, a portrait painter from a wealthy aristocratic Italian family. After that, Twombly more or less lived in Italy for the rest of his life.

In 1966 *Vogue* society photographer Horst P. Horst traveled to Rome to photograph the Twomblys in their apartment. The now iconic photos show the airy interiors of a palazzo, the patrician light of old world opulence—marble floors, white walls, gold chairs, marble busts, and stacked canvases—not unlike the more contemporary luminous interiors in Stanley Kubrick's *2001: A Space Odyssey*. "The Roman apartment where the Twomblys now live, with their six-year-old son, Alessandro, happens to be in a palazzo," reported the journalist who was there on assignment. "In certain quarters, where it is assumed that avant-garde American artists should live in avant-garde American discomfort, this relatively insignificant fact has led to Twombly being suspected of having fallen for 'grandeur,' and somehow betrayed the cause."

However, the trail Twombly was blazing as an artist was less a betrayal of the avant-garde than an entirely different path from the start. Unlike his contemporaries back in New York (including Rauschenberg) who were major forces in shaping the Pop and Minimal art scenes, Twombly was looking back in time, searching through history and culture, literature, and classical mythology, to make his work—he once described the individual lines he scratched onto his canvases, each one separated by soft white diaphanous space, as "the actual experience with its own innate history." In the catalogue to Twombly's 1979 exhibition at the Whitney Museum, *Cy Twombly: Paintings and Drawings 1954–1977*, Roland Barthes describes his paintings as "a sort of palimpsest, they give the canvas the depth of the sky in which light clouds pass in front of each other without blotting each other out." This quality is perhaps one reason why some have found in a number of Twombly's paintings echoes of the work of Arcadian painter Nicolas Poussin (1594–1665), who left Paris for the archaeological and mythological spirit of Rome ("I would have liked to be Poussin, if I'd had a choice, in another time," Twombly said in an interview with Nicholas Serota). Yet Poussin's sensuous depictions of narratives, like the birth of Venus or Bacchanalia, are not depicted by Twombly, but evoked by the power of their name. Barthes also advises the viewer not to seek analogy when Twombly inscribes his canvas *The Italians* (1961) with roughly written words like "to write The Italians is to see all Italians." The meaning merges with the act of announcing, of inscribing.

Canvases were taped to the gallery walls—an extension of Twombly's ethereal abode—before being violently attacked, then corrected with clouds of white and peeled off, a transference of Roman luminosity to major museums around the world. The invention and enactment of this process is reason enough for Twombly to have traveled to Italy.

Twombly Tapes a Canvas in Rome, after Horst P. Horst, 2013
$1\frac{3}{16} \times 1\frac{37}{64}$" (3 × 4 CM)

To re-examine a history

"To send architectural students to Rome is to cripple them for life," thundered Le Corbusier in *Vers une architecture*. Robert Venturi obviously begged to differ: "As a temporary expatriate, reveling in the baroque splendors of the city beyond my studio windows and steeping myself in the ambience of all Italy beyond the horizon, I was at the same time peculiarly sensible to a vision of my own land— visualizing old things in new ways and from different angles …

The American in Europe, especially the young artist, finding an American identity through absorbing a European heritage can be a most pompous cliché, but here I think it fits."

The Swiss architectural historian Martino Stierli has charted the young Robert Venturi's sojourns in postwar Italy as an update of the eighteenth-century Grand Tour initiation ritual. At that time, traveling to Europe to study architecture was tantamount to a rejection of the "no history" ontology of CIAM. Venturi's interest in the enclosed character of public space—a contextual reading—also ran counter to the modern orthodoxy of the building as a stand-alone object.

American Boys Go Grand Tour, Venturi and Twombly, 2012
$3^{15}\!/_{16} \times 4^{59}\!/_{64}$" (10 × 12.5 CM)

Venturi first visited Italy in the summer of 1948, after graduating from Princeton (whose "emphasis on history made it seem *démodé* in the postwar intellectual climate," Stierli writes). "I love it," he said in a letter home to his parents. "It is really very different from what I expected. There is so much color in the buildings against a deep blue sky and deep green foliage—something we who have lived in America cannot imagine." Desperate to return, he applied three times to the American Academy in Rome before he was finally accepted in 1954, with a little help from Louis Kahn. During his two-year fellowship Venturi made trips out of Rome—to his ancestral village in Atessa, to southern France and Barcelona, to the monastery of Certosa Ema that had so influenced Le Corbusier, as well as to Egypt and Greece, which was "wonderful," he said, "but it can't compare with Italy where every village is a masterpiece"—a clear rejection of Le Corbusier's white corporeal sunlit objects seen against a wide landscape in favor of Italy's complex urban ensembles that housed everyday life behind and in front of articulated facades. At the Academy Venturi encountered Pier Luigi Nervi (not without language difficulties) and also the postwar architectural discourse of the *neorealismo* movement, whose emphasis on variety, traditional materials, and the integration of existing buildings would result in the 1959 CIAM (Otterlo) attack on Ignazio Gardella's Casa alle Zattere and BBPR's Torre Velasca in Milan. Ernesto Rogers, a partner at BBPR and editor of *Casabella*, tutored at the Academy and took Venturi under his wing. According to Stierli, Rogers' parallel acceptance and rejection of modernism "resembles a characteristic trait in the architectural thinking of Venturi, whose stance equally [was] one of simultaneous alliance and dissociation from the established tenets of modernism." All of these experiences laid the foundation for Venturi's *Complexity and Contradiction in Architecture*, published in 1966. Indeed, Stierli argues that the outbreak of postmodernism that Venturi's publication set in motion was an Americanization of the *neorealismo* interest in popular architectural language. This and a preference for the complexities of baroque facades suggest a comparison between the Vanna Venturi House, built in Philadelphia in 1964, and Luigi Moretti's 1949 Casa il Girasole. Both explore the emancipation of the facade as surface of inscription, signification through an abstracted physiognomy.

To paint Hitler's favorite picture—
Traffic-island of the Dead

Just outside the fourteenth-century walls of Florence and the former Porta a Pinti, at the center of the Piazzale Donatello is a singular *isola sepolcrale*—an island of craggy trees encircled by traffic. Originally laid out in 1828 by the architect Carlo Reishammer for expired Swiss, the Cimitero degli Inglesi (English Cemetery) became the final resting place for the non-Catholics of Florence—1,409 dead writers, artists, and travelers from 16 countries who were, by law, denied a burial within the city walls. The Swiss symbolist painter Arnold Böcklin (1827–1901) kept a studio around the corner and made the island the subject of his haunting five-work masterpiece *Isle of the Dead* (1880–86). In place of a traffic ring were the midnight-ink waters of the River Styx giving way to a luminous island of cypress trees and burial chambers built into the jutting rock. Böcklin's Berlin art dealer gave the painting its title, but Böcklin himself preferred *Die Gräberinsel*, Tomb Island.

Traffic Island of the Dead, 2022
3 15/16 × 5 1/2" (10 × 14 CM)

176

The first *Isle of the Dead*, painted in 1880, hangs in the Kunstmuseum in Basel. A subsequent, smaller version painted on wood and completed the same year is in the Metropolitan Museum of Art in New York. This second work was commissioned by the widowed Marie Berna as a memorial to her husband. She had called the first *Isle* a "dream image," but for her painting she requested the addition of a coffin and female figure, interpreted by Böcklin as a standing form shrouded in white arriving by boat, both of which were subsequently painted into the first version and remained a fixture in later editions. On finishing the painting the artist wrote to Marie Berna, "now you can dream your way down into the world of shades."

Three years later Böcklin painted the third *Isle of the Dead*, inscribing his initials "AB" above a sepulcher cut into the rock. In 1884 the Dutch-born industrialist and art collector Baron Heinrich Thyssen commissioned a fourth version, which Böcklin's admirer, Adolf Hitler, eventually came to own. It hung in the Reich Chancellery in Berlin until it was destroyed during the Second World War. The fifth and final version was commissioned in 1886 by the Museum of Fine Art in Leipzig, where it still hangs.

But Böcklin did not repeat himself endlessly into old age (unlike another admirer, Giorgio de Chirico). Most likely it was the death of his infant daughter, whom he buried at the Cimitero degli Inglesi, which brought about a sea-change in his work. In 1888, the year she died, Böcklin kicked his *Gräberinsel* habit and painted *Die Lebensinsel* (Isle of Life), filled with optimistic symbolism: the island is now lush and green and peopled by youths at play, while naiads and swans frolic in the waters around it.

Böcklin's inspiration, with its grove of tall dark trees, is open to the public. In real life the water of the River Styx is actually asphalt — a sea of death for anyone who attempts to cross through the maelstrom of traffic. The artist may have taken the motif from a handful of other islands: Pontikonisi, a Greek islet near Corfu, or the archipelago of the Pontine Islands in the Tyrrhenian Sea. His vision of an arrival of coffins by boat happens daily at the enigmatic Isola di San Michele in the Venetian lagoon. The cemetery in Florence is today tended by Julia Bolton Holloway, an Englishwoman who welcomes visitors in Italian and maintains a library in the entrance pavilion for Roma people, who in turn help her maintain the grounds and assist in her utopian vision of reforming the ills of the contemporary world through chastity, study, prayer, and gardening.

To see a modern city

In June 1907 a 20-year-old Charles-Édouard Jeanneret (the future Le Corbusier, not to be confused with Charles Edward Jeanneret, the nineteenth-century Australian politician and pioneer of trams and steamboats) traveled with his friend Léon Perrin to Florence and Siena, where he cultivated an interest in the Middle Ages and motifs derived from nature—an influence that had percolated through his Ruskinian teacher Charles L'Eplattenier at the École d'Art, La Chaux-de-Fonds. In Florence he kept a room across from the Loggia dei Lanzi, where he sketched Donatello's *Judith and Holofernes*. On a visit to the fifteenth-century Certosa Ema in the Florence suburb of Galluzzo, Charles-Édouard was greatly impressed by the independence of the monks' living quarters. Each had a spartan bedroom, another room for praying, and access to a small secluded garden—an expressed and serialized cell module that added up to a coherent and communal building figure. Soon after, in 1910, he experimented with this system in a sketch for a pyramid of stacked ateliers.

The agile master visited the Certosa again in 1911, when returning to Switzerland from his *Voyage d'Orient* (published and mythologized in 1966), where he had pulled off an 18-day stay among the ascetics of Mount Athos. It was not only the frugality of monastic life that hypnotized him; in *Precisions: On the Present State of Architecture and City Planning* (1930) he recollects, "In the musical landscape of Tuscany I saw a modern city crowning a hill ... I thought I had never seen such a happy interpretation of dwelling ... This 'modern city' dates from the fifteenth century. Its radiant vision has always stayed with me." As Frederick Etchells notes in the introduction to the 1931 first English translation of *Vers une architecture*, "Mr Le Corbusier writes in a somewhat staccato style."

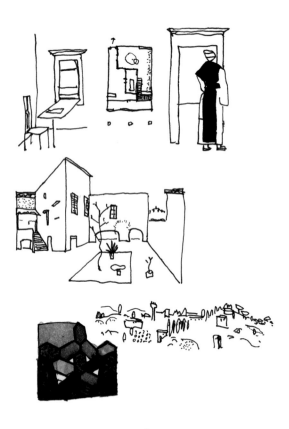

Certosa Ema, Florence, 2011
4 ¹¹⁄₁₆ × 3 ⁵⁄₃₂" (12 × 8 CM)

To die in Venice

In Thomas Mann's novella *Death in Venice*, published in 1911, the protagonist Gustav von Aschenbach—perhaps modeled on Richard Wagner, who died in Venice shortly after completing *Parsifal* in 1882— descends from the Apollonian to the Dionysian, expiring in his deck chair with a view of a toxic-gray Adriatic horizon from the Lido's Hotel Excelsior. In 1927 the exiled Russian impresario Sergei Diaghilev also stayed at the Excelsior. The entire Ballets Russes had been hired to entertain the guests at a party hosted by Cole Porter and his wife, the American socialite Linda Lee Thomas. Diaghilev, in return, was not so enthused by the new American music genre represented by Porter and his jazz troupe and checked out of the Excelsior in protest. "They are even teaching the Charleston on the Lido beach! It's dreadful!" he wrote to his pet secretary, the poet Boris Kochno, who, undeterred, promptly embarked on a passionate affair with Cole Porter. Diaghilev died in Venice two years later and was buried in the Orthodox section of the cemetery island of San Michele.

To play golf on the lido

A 53-year-old Winston Churchill, then British Chancellor of the Exchequer, traveled to Venice in 1927 in the company of his scientific advisor, Frederick Lindemann, 1st Viscount Cherwell, to investigate chemical plants in the new industrial zone of Porto Marghera—an enterprise supported by the multi-tasking Giuseppe Volpi. On learning of Churchill's imminent arrival and wanting to make a good impression, Volpi had a golf course constructed on the southern tip of the Lido.

Grand Hotel Excelsior + Bolles+Wilson,
Palazzo del Cinema (*far right*), Lido, Venice, 2013
2 × 11¹³⁄₁₆" (5 × 30 CM)

To be designated
persona non grata

"I get no kick from champagne / mere alcohol doesn't thrill me at all ... some get a kick from cocaine / I'm sure that if I took even one sniff / that would bore me terrific'ly too," sang Cole Porter, a little untruthfully. Porter hosted parties in Venice that were legendary for their spectacular nature (and debauchery). On one occasion he hired 50 gondoliers to serve as footmen, on another, tightrope walkers teetered above the heads of the guests. But it all became too much for the mayor of Venice, who instructed Porter to leave the city when a group of young Venetian men—who happened to include his nephew—were found dressed (if at all) in the ballgowns of the palazzo's owner, with a mountain of cocaine on the table.

To invent reasons for traveling to Italy

The American syndicated gossip columnist Elsa Maxwell, rumored to have been born during a performance of *Mignon* at an opera house in Keokuk, Iowa, made a name for herself staging scavenger and treasure hunts for the rich and famous. In the early 1920s the Italian tycoon Giuseppe Volpi (also founder of the Venice Film Festival), caught wind of Maxwell's talent as a professional party hostess and each summer hired her for two months to promote Venetian high life by bringing throngs of stars to his Hotel Excelsior. The Lido, which 30 years before had been wasteland, became the playground of the smart set. So pleased was Volpi with Maxwell's ability to put the Lido on the map that he convinced Mussolini to give her a medal for her services to Italian tourism. When asked to reflect on her success, Maxwell, who often said she felt "loved by 20 million people," summed it all up with "not bad, for a short, fat, homely piano player from Keokuk, Iowa, with no money or background, [who] decided to become a legend and did just that."

To explore the galaxy

When Mussolini invaded Albania in 1939 the deposed King Zog fled the country (with his fortune) and moved to the Ritz in London—an ignominious, but perhaps predictable, end to an Italo-Albanian alliance that had begun 12 years before. In 1927 Zog had been Zogu, a mere military dictator installed by an army of mercenaries (funded by international oil corporations). It was with Mussolini's approval that he elevated himself from president to king the following year, shortening his name to give it a more royal ring. For his coronation the streets of the capital Tirana were bedecked with Albanian flags—red with the black two-headed Skanderbeg eagle—imported en masse from Italy. For his 1938 marriage to a Hungarian countess Italian planes dropped confetti while Albanians on a six-day holiday binge lit bonfires and slaughtered countless sheep in front of Zog's palace. Fearful of poisonings, Zog preferred dinners cooked by his mother or eldest sister. Danger lurked everywhere, though one attempted assassination in Vienna ended with Zog enhancing his international reputation enormously by drawing a gun and firing back.

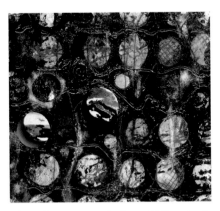

The Galaxy of Zog, Approached at an Oblique Angle, 2013
4 $^{11}/_{16}$ × 4 $^{11}/_{16}$" (12 × 12 CM)

In the 1930s, propelled by Zog's modernizing zeal, the center of Tirana was marshalled by a central axis planned by the Italian architects Florestano di Fausto and Armando Brasini in a refined rationalist style echoing the EUR in Rome. In 2003 Bolles+Wilson were one of three architects invited by Tirana's mayor Edi Rama to submit a masterplan updating the central axis precinct. Out of this came our Rationalist Apartment Building, completed in 2008, which terminates a cross-axis between the original Italian university and the adjacent rationalist art academy.

During construction it was noted from a Tirana–Malpensa night-flight that the fogbound Po Valley had evolved into a galaxy of illuminated jellyfish. These were not cities but asteroids of *la città diffusa*—a new star system of floating fragments, the city exploded and scattered across the landscape: space debris. Most likely Palladio's Teatro Olimpico lurks somewhere in there, a dark star in this galaxy of neon. The Teatro's ceiling also projects a dematerialized azure, a trope not dissimilar to the neon galaxy of the exploded city. This unlikely observation is in itself a reason to travel to Italy—or over Italy—in winter.

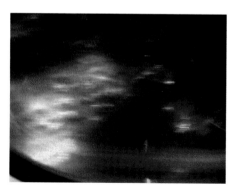

Illuminated Jellyfish: *La Città Diffusa* from the Air,
photo Peter Wilson, 2012

184

To attend a fascist youth camp

Colonia Workout, 2013
$1^{37}/_{64} \times 4^{11}/_{16}$" (4 × 12 CM)

As a boy growing up in Edinburgh, the Italo-Scottish sculptor Eduardo Paolozzi (a future member of the Independent Group, along with Reyner Banham and Alison and Peter Smithson) lived above his family's ice cream shop. His father thought Mussolini wonderful, and dispatched young Eduardo to a fascist boys' camp in Italy for his summer holidays. The 3,000 happy campers were each issued with a black shirt and an aluminum tumbler. They paraded the grounds with military priests, performed the *Alzabandiera* (flag-raising ceremony), and marched into a dining hall featuring a double life-size statue of *Il Duce*. Also on the agenda for the young campers were exercises in formation, fascist sing-alongs, Laurel and Hardy on an open-air cinema screen, and performances by swimsuit-clad dancers doing the tango. When Italy declared war on Britain on June 10, 1940, Eduardo, then 16, was interned for three months in Saughton prison. He never saw his father again. Paolozzi Sr had also been detained along with Eduardo's grandfather and uncle, and the three were among the 446 Italians who drowned when the ship carrying them to an internment camp in Canada was torpedoed by a German U-Boat.

After de Chirico's 1933 Set for Vincenzo Bellini's *The Puritans*, 2014
2 × 1³⁷⁄₆₄" (5 × 4 CM)

Set for Ildebrando Pizzetti's *Orseolo*, 2014
3 × 3¹¹⁄₃₂" (7.5 × 8.5 CM)

Sets and Costumes for Pietro Aschieri's *Nabucco*, 2014
3 × 3¹¹⁄₃₂" (7.5 × 8.5 CM)

To re-import a shadow

In the years between 1912 and 1914 Giorgio de Chirico painted his emblematic metaphysical art (*pittura metafisica*), the by now overfamiliar melancholy, uncertainty and enigmas of the hour, the poet, a street or a departure. The shadows that give these works their haunting aura are considered archetypically Italian (like the shadows of Aldo Rossi), but the pictures were painted in Paris.

Although his family was Italian, de Chirico spent his formative years in Greece and studied painting in Munich, where his decisive influences were a symbolist painter and a philosopher—Böcklin and Nietzsche, respectively. The latter wrote of "a strange and profound poetry, infinitely mysterious and solitary, based on the mood of an autumn afternoon when the weather is clear and the shadows are longer than in summer, for the sun is beginning to lower. Turin is the city where this extraordinary phenomenon is most apparent."

In 1912 de Chirico moved from Florence to Paris, making a quick pitstop in Turin to verify Nietzsche's profound observation. The Paris pictures, taken up by the surrealists, are an idealized "south of the Alps" painted "north of the Alps" and re-imported into Italy when de Chirico returned for military service in 1914. Or was it to re-import shadows (and the metaphysical movement—in his suitcase) that de Chirico traveled back to Italy?

Postscript: a trip to Turin to speak at the 2008 UIA conference seemed like a good opportunity to verify the Nietzsche shadow phenomenon, but the day was overcast and in any case a new species of media radiance and penumbra seemed to have eclipsed metaphysical shadow. On entering a large square at dusk one was met with the overwhelming sight of the pavement awash with seated onlookers gazing intently at one facade—a huge video projection screen. Cascading across this illuminating surface were speakers from UIA—Stefano Boeri, Joseph Rykwert, Italo Rota—architects who appeared here to have taken on an urban dimension. On closer inspection, however, these protagonists were to be found sitting directly below the media facade, a miniscule discussion panel. Suddenly my old chum, the ubiquitous Cino Zucchi, filled the screen (and filled the square with his eloquent effervescence)— the radiance of the architect/facade momentarily usurping the role of the enigmatic Turin shadow.

De Chirico's Suitcase, 2011
$4\,^{11}/_{16} \times 5\,^{29}/_{32}$" (12 × 15 CM)

To write your name in water

Travel to Italy became so popular after the end of the Napoleonic Wars that Byron in 1817 described Rome as "pestilent with English—a parcel of staring boobies, who go about gaping and wishing it to be at once cheap and magnificent." Keats' proto-Romantic friends, the Shelleys, arrived one year after that, crossing the Pass of Mont Cenis in March 1818. The collision between their expectations and reality caused Percy Bysshe Shelley to speculate that "there are two Italys ... one sublime and lovely; the other most degraded, disgusting, and odious."

Romanticism would revive the Elizabethan tradition of casting Italy as a hotbed of violence, incest, and hypocrisy, dense with dastardly dukes and contemptible intellectuals in the mold of the fiendish Machiavelli. This Romantic trope of the Italian villain was promoted in Gothic novels like Ann Radcliffe's 1794 *The Mysteries of Udolpho* or her 1797 *The Italian*, a genre that Byron termed "trash about Italy by writers who had never been there." "Stiletto School" writers were obsessed with knives (during the Napoleonic occupation the French had banned the carrying of stilettos, with little effect on the thriving cult of assassination). John Ruskin wrote to the Reverend Thomas Dale in 1840, "There is a strange horror lying over the whole city [Rome] which I can neither describe nor account for; it is a shadow of death, possessing and penetrating all things."

That shadow had already overtaken Keats in 1821, as he lay stricken with consumption at 26 Piazza di Spagna. His burial place below the daisies and wild violets of Monte Testaccio (a mound of broken antique amphorae) would inspire Oscar Wilde's poem "The Grave of Keats," with that most romantic of lines: "O poet-painter of our English Land! / Thy name was writ in water—it shall stand."

Lake Lugano, 1985

$3^{15}/_{16} \times 6^{19}/_{64}$" (10 × 16 CM)

Alps, 1986
$3\,^{15}/_{16} \times 3\,^{5}/_{32}$" (10 × 8 CM)

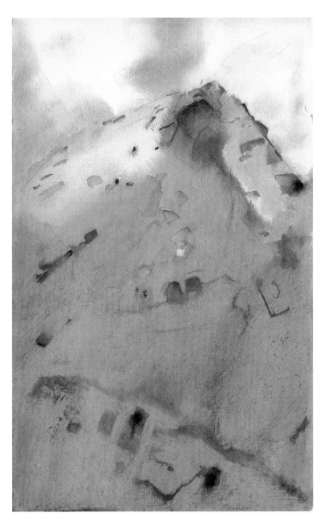

Alps, 1986

$3\,^{15}\!/_{16} \times 3\,^{5}\!/_{32}$" (10 × 8 CM)

Alps, 1986

$3^{15}\!/_{16} \times 3^{5}\!/_{32}$" (10 × 8 CM)

To be distracted by the Alps
while heading for Italy

For 25 years prior to his first Italian tour J. M.W. Turner (1775–1851) was infected by a fictitious Romantic Italy. In the absence of the real thing, he would sketch Italian subjects in the style of Claude Lorrain, or from descriptions in Eustace's *Classic Tours* and Byron's *Childe Harold*. When he came to make his own pilgrimage in 1819–20 he traveled, like the Shelleys the year before, via the Mont Cenis Pass. In a painting held by the Birmingham Museums and Art Gallery he depicts the crossing in a snowstorm maelstrom where everything is in movement. It is hard to imagine this as a prelude to Goethe's Arcadian *topos*—Italy as an idealized secular paradise in harmony with nature and divinities. A paradigm shift had taken place; Italy had become the goal of Romantic flight from the machine or, as in the case of Byron, the search for a cause to sacrifice oneself to. But the machine was not far behind. The 12km Mont Cenis tunnel between Savoy and Piedmont, providing direct railway passage from Paris to Rome, was constructed between 1857 and 1871. Next the Swiss, after deciding against the Splüngen option (the pass used by Nietzsche), got the Enterprise du Grand Tunnel du Gotthard underway: the southern portal was begun on September 13, 1872, the northern one a month later, on October 24.

The element air, which like Turner's painting denies materiality, was harnessed to penetrate the stone of the alpine massif. A construction company headed by the engineer Louis Favre developed and perfected a type of pneumatic drill that had been used first on the Mont Cenis tunnel. The machine drilled 1m-deep holes into the rock face for dynamite, the demand for which was so great that an explosives factory had to be constructed at nearby Urnersee. On February 28, 1880 a drill from the south tunnel broke through the rock face to the north tunnel, and on May 22, 1882 600 guests rode for the first time through the 15km tunnel from the north to the

Alps, 2002

$1 \times 10^{15}\!/\!_{64}$" ($2.5 \times 26$ CM)

south of the Alps, from Immensee to Chiasso. Favre was not on board: he had died in 1879 from heart failure at the 3km mark in his tunnel. Around 200 workers, most of them poor Italians from Piedmont and Lombardy, also died during construction, in miserable and dangerous working conditions. By 1897, when 61 trains a day traversed the tunnel, to spend 17–22 minutes under the Alps had become the principal "reason to travel to Italy."

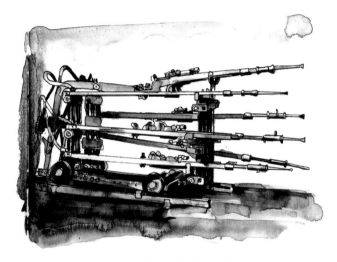

Pneumatic Drill, Gotthard Tunnel, 2014
$3^{15}\!/_{16} \times 5\,^1\!/_2$" (10 × 14 CM)

Via Mala: Sublime Terror, on the Way to the Splüngen Pass, 2008
5½ × 3¹⁵⁄₁₆" (14 × 10 CM)

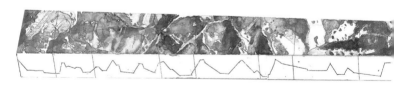

Alps Section and Yardstick, 2008
2 23/64 × 11 13/16" (6 × 30 CM) and 1 37/64 × 2 FT. 3 9/16 × 25/32" (4 × 70 × 2 CM)

To dream photography,
the pencil of nature

On his honeymoon in 1833 the gentleman scientist William Henry Fox Talbot (1800–1876) tried sketching Lake Como using a camera lucida. Dissatisfied with the experience, he set out to find a way to "cause these natural images to imprint themselves durably, and remain fixed upon the paper." In 1839, not wishing to be eclipsed by a certain Monsieur Daguerre, who had managed to freeze an image on a metal plate, Fox Talbot made public the results of five years of experimentation with his 16-page treatise, *Some Account of the Art of Photogenic Drawing*, or the *Process by which Natural Objects may be made to Delineate Themselves without the Aid of the Artist's Pencil*. Antonio Bertoloni, a botanist in Bologna with whom he had been corresponding for 13 years, received a copy of the treatise along with five packets containing examples of these photogenic drawings—some made by placing plants directly onto photosensitive paper, others printed from negatives made in a camera obscura, including a view of the grounds at the author's home, inscribed "Mio Gardino."

To meet one's Doppelgänger —
andare a zonzo

My Doppelgänger was wearing a black Milan T-shirt and space-shoes, items unknown in my wardrobe. He also wore The Tweed Suit (I'd been promised a second copy that never materialized). The Triennale preview overflowed with Milan design cognoscenti. Very few recognized us before the TV interview began. I did the talking; he just stood there off to my right, looking waxy. Although months before I had been diligently measured limb for limb and a team of Italian sculptors had been provided with comprehensive photo-documentation, his posture was something I have not yet and probably never will master. His hair was whiter and with an unfamiliar marzipan

Doppelgänger Anticipated, 2002–03

$3\frac{5}{32} \times 3\frac{5}{32}$" ($8 \times 8$ CM)

touch, but the resemblance was in any case closer than the neighboring Mannequin-Mendini, who appeared to have been born ten years after the original, or the radically slimline Dummy-Will-Alsop.

The TV interviewer asked in what way my Doppelgänger's costume—the Andare a Zonzo Suit—was a portrait of its author. The short answer is that I wanted it to be somewhat like a Bolles+Wilson building, robust on the outside with an unexpected material richness within. Robust in this instance meant tweed. English gentlemen climbers once attempted an ascent of Everest in three-piece tweed suits. My ideal garment also had to be warm—I come from a warm country (Australia), live in a cold one (Germany), and at that time worked in an inadequately insulated industrial building—and, more specifically, utilitarian, with a thin layer of padding stitched between tweed and lining, not just for its thermal value, but to make the whole quite stiff, volumetric, tube-like. The intention owes a certain allegiance not just to the worker's suit of the Chinese Cultural Revolution but to a degree-zero Joseph Beuys square-cut felt suit, without the aspiration to be a walking artwork. Erik Satie once purchased seven identical gray velvet corduroy suits and for the rest of his life his appearance in public never varied. Jim Stirling's blue shirts were similarly part of a uniform. The particular tweed that I had specified was more directly autobiographical; it was already hanging in my wardrobe in the form of a jacket bought in a second-hand shop in London more than 20 years ago. This is not at all your average English Colonel's herringbone, but a rather racy rough woven 1950s number with scattered colored flecks requalifying the traditional cultural codification of tweed—Highland-Pollock. I have a strong suspicion the fabric my Doppelgänger sported was more Chinese than Scottish in origin.

A certain lack of commitment in my Doppelgänger's stance could be explained by his relative inexperience. He was supposed to clutch his upper lapel and aggressively, even somewhat illicitly, open his jacket like a flasher or a black-market watch seller to reveal ... the jacket's patchwork lining, in a sensual warm pink red-brown that contrasted starkly with the suit's sensible and utilitarian exterior. Such an interior/ exterior dialectic characterizes the buildings of Loos, but in this instance its origins were closer to home—I have an Indian vest in my wardrobe in rough woven cotton, dark blue on the outside and a patchwork of reds and pinks within. Every time I glimpse it I'm reminded of the wall tapestries Le Corbusier designed for Chandigarh.

Andare a Zonzo Suit, 2002–03
$2^{23}\!/_{64} \times 3^{5}\!/_{32}$" (6 × 8 CM)

Interview over, the spotlight moved on to other contributors to the "Dressing Ourselves" exhibition—artists, designers, musicians, and architects brought together by Alchimia guru Alessandro Guerriero and modeled not in wax but in glass resin by Attilio Tono of Atelier Almayer. Each contributor had been asked to design a costume, a self-image. The American musicians Aluminum Group took the opportunity to become Gingerbread Men; architects Hariri and Hariri donned digital gear, and UN Studio a wrap of colored zippers with multiple opportunities for painful misuse. To our mutual relief my Doppelgänger and I soon parted to pursue our independent trajectories. Hopefully at other stations on his global tour the title of the suit will be correctly translated: *Andare a Zonzo—Herumbummeln*—Hanging out.

To enter Rome along the Appian Way

American Allied troops entered Rome in 1944 along the ancient Appian Way, whose sepulchers and noble insignia still spoke of solemn processions and triumphal entries even after centuries of plundering. As was his habit, Curzio Malaparte claimed the credit for this dramatic staging. In *The Skin* he reports that, as the liaison officer for the Allied forces, he personally had advised the American commander General Cork to enter Rome along the Via Appia Antica rather than the Via Appia Nuova: "It's a longer route, but it's more picturesque." The general had asked which road the Caesars had used to enter Rome and Malaparte smartly informed him that Marius, Sulla, Julius Caesar, Cicero, Pompey, Antony, Cleopatra, Augustus, and Tiberius had all preceded the US Army's Sherman tanks. Riding alongside the general, the learned guide pointed out the tombs of the noblest Roman families: "Gee!," shouted the gum-chewing GIs as they covered the ancient stones with their autographs. (Hollywood would appreciate their magnificence too, making them privileged backdrops for spectacular 1950s costume dramas along the lines of *Ben Hur*—films known in Italy as the "Sword and Sandal" genre.) From the summit of the grassy Tomb of the Horatii, with its romantic umbrella pines and cypresses in the manner of Poussin or Böcklin, the invading army scanned the roofs, cupolas and marble statues of Rome, the pyramidal tomb of Caius Cestius, the crenellated tower of the Mausoleum of Caecilia Metella (which appears in the background of Tischbein's *Goethe in the Roman Campagna*). Next the Allies passed the Quo Vadis church. "Where are you going?," Malaparte helpfully translated. "What? To Rome, of course!," the perplexed general shouted above the roar of tanks.

To photograph Genius Loci
in black and white

Christian Norberg-Schulz's 1979 *Genius Loci: Towards a Phenomenology of Architecture* rescued the latent poetry of architecture from the one-dimensionality of functionalism, presenting building as a means to achieve an "existential foothold." Of the 300 photographs in the book, 124 were taken in Italy. Translated into many languages, *Genius Loci* instigated a paradigm shift in architecture, a new validation of the historic city, of Italian cities in particular, and of the layering of time embodied in cumulative and generic structures. Almost universally, it led to a rescripting of urban planning.

On revisiting this milestone of a book in the age of digital excess, the overall impression is of a black-and-white world, but not of a world lacking in depth. The formatting modality of carefully cropped and edited photographs transmits both the poetry of place and an urgency, a revolutionary charm (as did the publication, 15 years earlier, of *Architecture Without Architects* by Bernard Rudofsky, or the layouts of Le Corbusier's *Oeuvre Complète*). From a distance of 30 years, this conspiratorial consistency seemed to demand a new mapping, a scanning that would take in the entire Norberg-Schulz form of visibility, its taxonomy, as a single matrix—an act of appropriation. The exercise of summarizing all the black-and-white plates on two pages of a sketchbook is not unlike Jorge Luis Borges' reduction of the conceptual structure of 400-page epic novels to a minimum number of lines. For only then does their overriding "fatal hue" (to borrow a phrase John Updike used to describe overlaid transparencies) emerge.

Genius Loci I, after Christian Norberg-Schulz, 2009
3½ × 4¹¹⁄₁₆" (9 × 12 CM)

209

Genius Loci II, after Christian Norberg-Schulz, 2009

$3\frac{1}{2} \times 4\frac{11}{16}$" ($9 \times 12$ CM)

To win the woodland cemetery competition

They're a real nuisance, the dead. They are jealous, and full of envy, and they forgive the living everything save the fact that they are alive... boot them to the cemetery and to hell with it.

Curzio Malaparte, *The Skin*, 1949

Both Erik Gunnar Asplund (1885–1940) and Sigurd Lewerentz (1885–1975) went on their own versions of the Grand Tour shortly before their youthful victory in the prestigious competition for a new cemetery in the south of Stockholm. Lewerentz traveled to Italy via Germany and a two-year apprenticeship in Munich (1907–09), where he would have become familiar with burial reform and with Hans Grässel's innovative designs for woodland cemeteries. His Italian travels in 1913–14—self-financed and self-initiated—allowed him to further an interest in vernacular buildings and their relationship to landscape that had been nurtured by his teacher, the national romanticist Ragnar Östberg. His diary records visits to the Greek theater at Syracuse—"the open space with the heavens above ... the stage, the plain, and the sea"—and to the Concord temple at Girgenti, "a wonderful spot chosen with an infinite sense of feeling." The Palazzo Pitti he describes as "delightfully simple and so enormously strong."

Whereas Asplund produced copious notes and sketches on his tour, Lewerentz did not sketch in Italy but relied on his camera. His photographs (now researched and theorized by Luis M. Mansilla) are radically edited ways of seeing, enigmatic in the extreme, textures and details formatted with "an anxious proximity to the frame"— as in a close-up fragment of the Palazzo Pitti wall (a materialization of its "so enormously strong" quality), or an abstract field of ancient mosaic with a classical leg dangling from the top.

Significant are the widely contrasting modes of documentation employed by the future partners: Lewerentz's radical minimalist glance (or was it an instant and selective editing down to a material

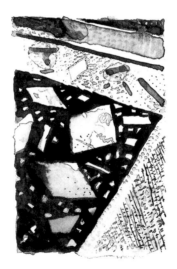

Syracuse Facade, after Erik Gunnar Asplund
and his postcard of Via delle Tombe, Pompeii, 2014
$2 \times 1^{37}/_{64}$" (5×4 CM) and $2^{23}/_{64} \times 1^{3}/_{8}$" ($6 \times 3.5$ CM)

essence, an indifference to convention), in contrast to Asplund's cumulative 300 sheets of sensuous drawings, sketches, notes, and portraits, along with 800 postcards to supplement his own photographs. Lewerentz's photographic selections of significant fragments prioritize "technical reproducibility" (Walter Benjamin's essentially modern recalibration of the relationship between subject and object). The Italy they describe is rendered modern, as far removed from the tradition they re-format as Ishimoto's abstracted compositions of Japanese gardens would be 50 years later.

Mega-rustication, Palazzo Pitti, 2022
$3\frac{5}{32} \times 3\frac{5}{32}$" ($8 \times 8$ CM)

How did the Italian experience of Asplund and Lewerentz inform the radical Woodland Cemetery design? We can see its influence firstly in the format of drawings submitted in May 1915, in the smudgy and atmospheric plan which co-opted existing site conditions (gravel quarries, station entrance). This plan would evolve (between 1916 and 1940) around a central axis, one that ultimately shed its south-side enclosure to reveal the loaded asymmetry of the Way of the Cross, the path to Asplund's Monumental Porch sublimely counterbalanced by an open and owing landscape with tree-crowned knoll (Lewerentz's landscaping revealing over time the temperament of the site).

Paving and stone bench, after photographs by Sigurd Lewerentz, 2014
1⅜ × 2¹¹⁄₆₄" (3.5 × 5.5 CM) and 2¹¹⁄₆₄ × 1⅜" (5.5 × 3.5 CM)

Further competition pages could well be from a travel sketchbook, each documenting specific moments, a sequence of spatial subplots, described not in their planimetric geometries but through atmospheric vignettes, an empathic placing of the viewer deep inside a Nordic forest of archaic burial rituals: "a Columbarium court," "graves in glades," or "the Urn Walk"—a deep dark fissure in the foliage. On one of the competition sheets, studies of forest graves were scrubbed onto three photos of the actual forest, giving a documentary and photographic verisimilitude to the intended atmosphere of archaic melancholy. This is a regional adaptation of Italian precedents, echoing the deep shadows in an Asplund postcard of Pompeii's Via delle Tombe or the ritual stations of north Italian *Sacri Monti* processional routes. The choreographed spatial sequencing of the cemetery buildings, completed by 1940, also finds a precedent in Asplund's Italian sketches (Syracuse facade), while a persistent and pensive materiality brings us back to Lewerentz's selective focusing technique. The landscape of the Woodland Cemetery, the product of Lewerentz's hand, is populated by small incidents in stone, fragments, isolated details like his Italian photos; even the mosaic floor of his sublime Resurrection Chapel could almost be of Pompeiian origin. Asplund also subsequently reverted to the Pompeiian, with the lush red interior ambience in his 1922–23 Skandia Cinema in Stockholm.

To re-format and become a first modern

It is said that on the day in 1911 when Wright's Wasmuth Portfolio was published in Berlin, work stopped in the atelier of Peter Behrens, where Jeanneret, Mies, and Gropius were all apprentices. The publication—colloquially named after its German publisher—was officially titled *Ausgeführte Bauten und Entwürfe von Frank Lloyd Wright* (Studies and Executed Buildings of Frank Lloyd Wright). Containing 100 lithographs covering 20 years of previously unpublished and largely unknown work, the anthology was arranged in two grand volumes. No distinction was made between built and unbuilt projects.

On the inside pages the graphic style was much influenced by the elegant Japanese renderings of Wright's assistant, Marion Mahony (who with her husband Walter Burley Griffin, another member of the Wright office, would go on to design the masterplan for the Australian capital Canberra). However, many projects were also redrawn by Wright and his son Lloyd while they were based in Florence in 1909 and 1910—a significant phase in the architect's career, and one that suggests his emergence on the Continent involved far more American Prairie/Central European crossovers than Wright's own self-mythologizing allowed. Indeed, after Italy he remained in Europe, traveling to Darmstadt to see Joseph Maria Olbrich (a visit cut short by Olbrich's untimely death) and to Vienna, where the *Wiener Secession* had emerged ten years earlier. Traces of these influences can be identified in many of the Wasmuth illustrations, notably the echoes of Josef Hoffmann in Wright's redrawn and abstracted suburban Illinois houses, even if Wright created a smokescreen to disguise their importance by praising in his introduction only the historically more distant Italian masters—Giotto, Arnolfo, Pisano, Brunelleschi, and Bramante, Sansovino and Michelangelo.

Yet elsewhere in this text Wright subscribed to the cause of emerging European modernism by parodying his American colleagues: "Brown calls for Renaissance, Smith for French Chateau Style, Jones for an English gentleman's house, Robinson for North German Hanseatic, and Hammerstein for Rococo," an obviously displeasing eclecticism that led him to trumpet his own mission— "reaction was unavoidable"—and he followed the one American architect worth pursuing, Louis Sullivan, in establishing a new aesthetic of his own.

The signature organicism of this aesthetic is particularly evident in the Wasmuth drawings of the Clooney, Thomas, Hartley, Tomek, and Robie houses. Writing in a later 1986 facsimile edition of the portfolio, the critic Vincent Scully noted how "the thin lines stretch across the predominantly empty pages as if out of some primal emptiness." The same emptiness is also visible in the plates dedicated to the Gerts House, where apart from a few orbiting trees Wright erases all of the context, so that the collision of its intersecting forms appears to float in space (much like Palladio's villas in his *Four Books*). It was precisely this abstraction that seized the European imagination. Take away a few of Wright's corners, for example, and in a stripped down Gerts House you can find the radicalism of Mies's 1924 brick Krefeld houses.

Those plans redrawn in Florence all exhibit this tendency. In house after house the central composition drifts off into empty space. Perhaps Wright's reason to travel to Italy was therefore to distance himself—not only from his Chicago life and family, but also from his already well-rehearsed compositional tropes in favor of a new, neutralized discursive space. The Florentine reformatting was not without consequence.

To abandon a bikini

The epic saga of Ulysses' wandering—a monumentally frustrated 10-year return from Troy to Ithaca—functions as a 3,000-year-old template for all subsequent journeying. Jean-Luc Godard's 1963 classic *Le Mépris* (*Contempt*), based on Alberto Moravia's novel *Il Disprezzo* (originally published in English as *A Ghost at Noon*, 1954), unfolds from this template, with the mythic Villa Malaparte as both protagonist and backdrop for characters that slip in and out of various Homeric guises: Brigitte Bardot transmutes from wife Penelope to nymph Calypso—black wig to blonde bombshell—as she traverses her marital quarters asking "Where is the man I married?," before becoming a Siren and swimming off, naked, in the direction of the Galli (appropriately, the actual Siren Rocks are visible from the villa's rooftop deck). Fritz Lang—playing himself as a famous director making a film of *The Odyssey*—jumps into the persona of the Emperor Tiberius on the cliffs of Capri when he questions the abandoned Penelope's fidelity. Michel Picoli, cast as Bardot's scriptwriter husband is, like Ulysses, under Calypso's spell (but in a cathartic homecoming reverts to the role of author—Homer). In the final scene, Godard himself appears on camera, calls for silence, and with Lang assumes joint command of the Villa Malaparte and its wide horizon.

Here the villa is a catalyst and a locus for symbolic transfers—best demonstrated in the relationship between its actual owner, who changed his name from Kurt Suckert to Curzio Malaparte (a play on Bonaparte), and the house he had built in his image—"*casa come me.*" How much influence the architect Adalberto Libera exerted on its design is not clear. When Field Marshall Rommel passed by on his way to North Africa and enquired whether the house was built or bought, Malaparte answered: "The severe cliffs of the Matromania, the giant rocks of the Faraglioni, the Sorrento peninsula, the blue Amal beach, the shores of Paestum shining behind it—all these are scenes that I designed."

Brigitte Bardot Sunbathes on the Roof of the Villa Malaparte
Wearing only a Book, 2014
$2\,^{23}\!/_{64} \times 2\,^{9}\!/_{16}$" (6 × 6.5 CM)

The Ulysses trope—journeyman, suffering hero, adaptive trickster—may provide an analogous role model for today's "star architect," journeying to the end of the world, to the underworld even, to China to construct a new city, a stadium, a TV station. What did Ulysses construct along the way? A horse, a raft, and a bed. From these three artifacts we could assume that like Daedalus or Hephaestus he was adept in *techne*—the act of making wondrous objects to overcome the disorder of the world, objects embodying *métis*, the inanimate becoming magically alive, not representing, but reproducing life.

To hang about

Just "hanging about" has long been an Italian pastime as visitors to the 1963 Fiera di Milano (Trade Fair) were able to attest when they witnessed a practical demonstration of the latest in building site safety. Although the demonstration embodied sinister memories it also turned to practical advantage national traumas relating to Mussolini's fate. The same principle was again thematized in the context of *arte povera*, when Luciano Fabro (sandwiched between Lawrence Weiner and Bruce Nauman in Germano Celant's iconic 1969 book) suspended aloft an inverted silhouette of Italy itself.

Just Hanging Around, 2022
2 × 2²³⁄₆₄" (5 × 6 CM)

Fiera di Milano, 1963

Luciano Fabro, *Italia*, 1969

To see Naples and die

The last line of Walter Benjamin's first metropolitan text, *Vedi Napoli e poi muori*, turns this old Italian adage into a pun, offering the city as the last thing one must do before dying or merely the first, before moving on to the nearby settlement of Mori. Benjamin himself had moved on to Italy in 1924, relocating from Berlin to the island of Capri, where he stayed with his friend Ernst Bloch. It was here that he met the Latvian actress and theater director Asja Lacis, a Bolshevik known for her proletarian theater troupes for children. Lacis soon became his lover and collaborated with him on the essay "Naples," the first of his *Denkbilder* (thought–images) texts on urban life, which would be followed by "Moscow" in 1927, "Marseilles" in 1928, and his canonical 1927–40 Paris "Arcades Project" (*Passagenwerk*).

Echoing E. M. Forster's *A Room with a View*, Benjamin warns that in Naples even Baedeker cannot assist the unresourceful tourist. "Here the churches cannot be found, the starred sculpture always stands in the locked wing of the museum, and the word "mannerism" warns against the work of native painters." He goes on to challenge each of the city's component histories, characterizing its Pompeiian antiquity as a "swindle," its poverty as "contagious," and reports of the city's wonders as "fantastical" ("in reality it is gray: a gray-red or ochre, a gray-white"). Oscillating between the roles of archaeologist, collector, and detective, he gives us a portrait of the city that is all the more compelling for this unveiling.

What Benjamin exposes is a vertical topography of "innumerable, simultaneously animated theaters"—hermit's caves, cellars, and fishermen's taverns cut into the rocks, with seven-story tenements and cliff-top villas rising above them. Everything that is joyful is mobile—music, toys, ice-cream, even the condensed yet scattered world of fiesta fireworks. In this sense the magnetism of the city that Benjamin and Lacis mine is both beautiful and bestial. Similarly, like history itself, the metropolis is both destructive and redemptive. These parallel qualities are conveyed through writing that is fragmentary, emphasizing a city that is fundamentally porous—in its permeable architecture ("building and action interpenetrating in the courtyards, arcades and stairways"), in its unfolding of time ("irresistibly the festival penetrates each and every working day"), in its lack of clear boundaries between phenomena ("the permeation of the city by Catholic ritual").

In many ways, Benjamin's and Lacis' "Naples" precedes the fatal hue of Curzio Malaparte's postwar portrait of the same city in *The Skin* (1949). Both map intimate and often grotesque grains, specific moments within the labyrinthine structure of this palimpsest city. But while Malaparte's prose is a cynical, almost hysterical denigration of defeat, Benjamin's is only ever defined by its heightened *Anschaulichkeit* (clarity), crystallizing small moments that embody the total event in the city, in history.

To skate dangerously

The Polish artist Alina Szapocznikow (1926–1973) proposed filling the crater of Mount Vesuvius with ice to create a giant skating rink. To the strains of suitable piped music—"Russian waltzes like *On the Hills of Manchuria*"—skaters would circle the illuminated rink, defiantly playing where the "earth once spewed out infernal fire through its open entrails." If their defiance happened to be cut short by a sudden eruption in the midst of a figure-skating competition, that too formed part of a plan. "Fixed for eternity like Pompeiians," the astonished spectators and the skaters caught mid-pirouette would bear testament to the fleeting, futile nature of human existence.

The project was one of nine in a 1973 exhibition, *Operazione Vesuvio*, curated by the Paris art critic and regular *Domus* columnist Pierre Restany (1930–2003) and shown at the Galleria Il Centro in Naples.

To build a pavilion at the
Milan Triennale

The Catalan architect Josep Antoni Coderch (1913–1984) journeyed to Italy in 1951 as creator of the Spanish Pavilion at the IX Triennale in Milan. The 70m² U-shaped installation was defined by three walls— one made of timber shutters for viewing a grid of black-and-white photographs of Ibizan vernacular architecture and Gaudí details, another painted strawberry pink, another cobalt blue. This intense polychromy was further emphasized by up-lighting and punctuated by a foreground of numerous hovering craft objects, utensils and modern artworks, including a painting by Joan Miró. The only color photograph that exists was published in Luigi Moretti's *Spazio* magazine. Coderch reported that in Milan many participants said they were pleased to be dealing with Spaniards, even if they were representing the Franco regime. The pavilion's projection of depth and rich anthropological atmosphere attracted interest from Max Bill, who had designed the slick industrial aesthetic of the Swiss Pavilion. Further gestures of camaraderie came from Ernesto Rogers, Jean Prouvé, Aldo van Eyck, and Gio Ponti. Coderch and the pavilion's success—it won a Gold Medal and a Grand Prize—represented Spain's coming out into the world of postwar modernism.

Coderch in Milan, 2021
1 ^{37}/64 × 5 ^{29}/32" (4 × 15 CM)

Speakers at the 1951 Milan Triennale, 2008
$8^{17}/_{64} \times 1^{3}/_{8}$" (3.5 × 21 CM)

To experience the birth of arte povera

In 1967 Germano Celant published a manifesto in *Flash Art* calling for a new way to experience art and life. His "Notes for a Guerrilla" gave the artist the role of alchemist, one who discovers the essence of things in this world—copper, earth, water, lead, snow, grass, electricity, growth—and distils them into new compounds and solutions. Celant defined this work under a new rubric, *arte povera* (poor art), to mark a distinction from the contemporary valences of conceptual art, earthworks, anti-form, and impossible art.

Two years later Celant consolidated the manifesto with a book published first by Gabriele Mazzotta, Milan and then by Ernst Wasmuth, Tübingen. The book presented text and photographic documentation as a facet of the work itself, a direct experience requiring no further critical interpretation. One grainy black-and-white photograph shows a challenged public confronting Michelangelo Pistoletto's 1967–68 *Golden World*, a sphere "that first went through the streets and then came in a cage."

Emblematic of *arte povera* are igloos by Mario Merz—Celant's book included two—one in yellow clay and neon (height 1.2m, diameter 2m) and another accompanied by "a small thought for Celant—the broken window panes are the violinists, the spears are the organ, the sheaves have a beautiful sound, what more do you want?"

Further grainy photos show Alighiero Boetti's bound bunches (2.8m wide) of painted sticks as well as works by: Richard Long, Joseph Beuys, Robert Smithson, Barry Flanagan, Dennis Oppenheim, Joseph Kosuth, Bruce Nauman, Jannis Kounellis ("I would paint a farm house in the Roman Campagna deep blue, also inside"), Eva Hesse ("I would like the work to be non-work"), and Richard Serra (rubber 1967, lead 1968).

To be buried on a small island

Charles Perrott (1677–1706) of Northleigh was in Padua in October 1704 and Rome in 1705. In November 1706 it was reported that he had died in Venice "following a very violent fever and was buried next day on a small island."

Perrot's Small Island, Reinstated, 2013
$2\,^{23}\!/_{64} \times 5\,^{29}\!/_{32}$" (6 × 15 CM)

To recover after
your house has exploded

In 1874 a gunpowder-laden barge on Regent's Canal exploded, blowing the front off Townshend House, home to the painter Lawrence Alma-Tadema (1836–1912). The drama prompted the artist to retreat with his family to Rome and Naples for the winter. But this was not Alma-Tadema's first London house explosion, nor was this his first wife to accompany him on a trip to Italy.

After Alma-Tadema I, 2015
$1^{37}/_{64} \times 3^{5}/_{32}$" (4 × 8 CM)

After suffering a nervous breakdown as a teenager Lawrence Alma-Tadema (born Lorens Tadema) was advised by doctors to spend what little time they believed he had left doing what brought him pleasure. This meant learning genre painting at the Antwerp Academy of Art, forgoing his father's wish that he study law. A visit to the marble-lined smoking room of a gentleman's club in Ghent awoke his interest in the depiction of marble. While his early efforts were less than successful—his teacher Henri Leys criticized them for looking like cheese—Tadema spent the rest of his life correcting this painful material ambiguity. Towards the end of his highly successful career *Punch* described him as a "Marbelous" painter, suggesting he become a KCMB (Knight of the Cool Marble Bath).

After Alma-Tadema II, 2015
2¾ × 1³⁄₁₆" (7 × 3 CM)

In 1863 Tadema married Pauline Gressin. They honeymooned in Italy, where he sketched Pompeii and visited marble quarries. Three years later, on a visit to London, a gas explosion rocked the house in St John's Wood in which they were staying. Pauline's nerves never recovered from the shock and she died in 1869. The following year Tadema returned to London, this time to settle, partly forced out of Europe by the outbreak of the Franco-Prussian War, partly drawn by the lure of the 18-year-old Laura Epps, who would soon become his second wife. A stroke of inspiration—adding his middle name to his surname—moved him up from the lower rankings to the top of the alphabetical exhibition catalogues. He was taken up by the London market, his commercial success based almost exclusively on depicting scenes of ancient Rome in which the young maidens bore a striking resemblance to the daughters of the British bourgeoisie—thus flattering British imperial aspirations while also reflecting the luxuries of Victorian upper middle-class life. Tadema's themes—as in *Expectations, From an Absent One*, or *In the Tepidarium*—sometimes verged on soft porn. Carefully avoiding any myth or allegory that might overtax his client, they emphasized instead the Victorian values of home, family, idealized love as well as indolence, complacency and materialism. He bathed his subjects and his clients in Italian light, giving them Italian air to breathe.

Alma-Tadema Measures in Pompeii, 2015
5 3/32 × 5 3/32" (13 × 13 CM)

Ruskin, Wilde, and Sargent all loathed his work and its exploitation of the market. "Sly Alma, what does he know of my hangings," Whistler wrote in the *Pall Mall Gazette*. "His Romano-Dutch-St John's-Wooden Eye has never looked upon them! ... Tadema boom da ay!!" St John's Wood was the location of the £70,000 house that Tadema bought at the height of his success in the 1880s. Casa Tadema was a collision of styles: Golden Age Dutch (including a Vermeer for Mrs Tadema) ploughing into High Victorian and ancient Roman—a real-life manifestation of one of his paintings. The eclectic décor included a studio with a ceiling of polished aluminum (then a rare metal), a mosaic atrium of sea-green Siena marble and solid cast-bronze doors—replicas of those in the House of Eumachia in Pompeii. Enrico Caruso, Dame Nelly Melba, and even Tchaikovsky performed at house parties, playing on a piano held together by LT monogrammed screws.

Tadema's work was characterized by archaeologically correct obsessive detail, informed by photographs of ruins and winters spent in Italy sketching coastlines around the Bay of Naples. His signature motif was of pining nymphs on white marble benches, suspended breathtakingly high above a deep blue Mediterranean. The Tadema Victorians-in-togas style subsequently provided a visual language for Hollywood "Sword and Sandal" epics.

To witness fascism

Italy, and in particular the Italian Renaissance, was the focus of a lifetime's engagement by the art historian Aby M. Warburg (1866–1929). Spending long periods in Florence and Rome, he spoke perfect Italian, though the experience of the First World War somewhat cooled his ardor: a true German patriot, he believed Germany would have won had it not been not for the Italians. After the war he spent four years in the Bellevue Sanatorium in Switzerland, recovering from a nervous breakdown (which was eventually cured by opium treatment and his own written analysis of a Hopi snake dance he had seen in New Mexico many years before). Back in Hamburg in 1924, Warburg embarked on his last project, the *Mnemosyne Atlas*, a psycho-historic system of image association designed to map the "afterlife of Antiquity"—or its continual re-emergence and reanimation in later eras, in the form of images of great symbolic, emotional, and intellectual power. In his last years, too, he set off again for Italy, accompanied by his assistant Gertrude Bing. Together they kept an extensive travel diary recording encounters with artworks and Italian colleagues.

Traveling rekindled Warburg's affection for Italy. It also gave him a new role, charting the seismic changes of an epoch. In Bologna on September 28, 1928 Warburg met Professor Lorenzo Bianchi, who painted a rosy picture of developments in Italy following the 1922 Fascist March on Rome. Bianchi absolved Mussolini of any blame for the 1924 murder of the socialist leader Giacomo Matteotti, and claimed that the fascists were implementing the ideals of the French Revolution. Further encounters in academia brought Warburg to the conclusion that Bianchi's narrative was a university professor's obligatory acquiescence. The five killers of Matteotti—all of them unambiguously linked to Mussolini—were arrested, but freed in a 1925 amnesty for political prisoners. That Warburg was aware of these events is confirmed by an entry in his diary from March 1929, when he notes that he had traveled along the Lungotevere Arnaldo da Brescia, "the place where Matteotti was murdered." In Rome he had meetings in quick succession with Ernst Steinmann—Michelangelo expert and director of the Bibliotheca Hertziana, whose office was adorned with a portrait of Mussolini—and with the art historian Arduino Colasanti, an outspoken anti-fascist.

In a diary entry from the previous month, Warburg relates that he had been to the cinema and seen a film of the *Conciliazione*—the ceremonial unifying of the Holy See and the fascist state. He describes the memorable moments—the pomp as Pope Pius XI climbed into a glamorous new car, and an astounding close-up of Mussolini's evilly beautiful Caesar-like lip movement (a magic effect akin to that of the Hopi shaman). With an art historian's eye, Warburg selected for his *Mnemosyne Atlas* two newspaper photographs of Cardinal Gasparri and the *Duce* signing the accord between Church and Dictator. Another image destined for the *Atlas* was a postage stamp emblazoned with a bundle of birch rods (*fasces*).

On returning to Hamburg Warburg concluded his diary notes by describing the fascist regime as "*italo-catholic*" and as a menacing monster. The photos of the Cardinal and the *Duce* remain in the Atlas without interpretive text, as Warburg died not long after, on October 29, 1929.

To don Tuscan glasses

Giuseppe Zocchi's 1744 *Vedute delle ville, e d'altri luoghi della Toscana*, published with the tourist market in mind, were designed to "set before the eyes of curious observers, especially foreign, the most noble and charming views." Still today they deliver historic scenes, Medici sets for contemporary visitors to imagine themselves in. Zocchi thematized the sumptuous ripples and folds of Tuscan topography, each bump crowned with its grand villa. As this characteristic landscape stretches out southwards into wide undulating swells, hills are capped instead with rustic farmhouses, lines of cypresses leading up to them—the iconic image of the holiday villa industry, each now rustically restored and garnished with a shining blue pool. Visitors today don Tuscan glasses that filter out infrastructural invasions and the parasitic fungi of just-in-time shopping centers, distribution sheds, the plague of the *città diffusa*. Curiously, a Tuscan *dérive* under the strict guidance of a GPS dominatrix involves a similar editing. Signora Tom-Tom's rotating maps are stripped of their third dimension, characteristic Tuscan ripples and folds flattened for "prepare to turn left" efficiency. What to do? Set the Tuscan glasses on reverse? Embarrass the lady by documenting her inadequate representation of the incident-laden panorama unfolding through the windshield?

Downsized Villa Medici at Poggio a Caiano, 2010
2⁹⁄₁₆ × 2" (6.5 × 5 CM)

Speeding Through Tuscany I, 2013
$1\,^{37}\!/_{64} \times 5\,^{29}\!/_{32}$" ($4 \times 15$ CM)

Would this constitute a subversive inflation of the topography, a grafting back onto Tuscany of an overlay of postcard expectations?

Of Zocchi's list of imposing villas dotted around Tuscan hilltops, the following are accessible today:

MEDICI VILLAS

— Villa dell'Ambrogiana, now an institute for psychiatric illness.
— Villa di Artimino, now an archaeological museum.
— Villa di Poggio a Caiano, a Medici summer residence (Cosimo's honeymoon hideaway) designed by Giuliano da Sangallo. The pedimented portico is perhaps the first Renaissance revival of an antique temple front. This villa provided the model for subsequent Renaissance re-enactments of antique villas described by Vitruvius and Pliny. Victor Emmanuel II transformed the *piano nobile* ballroom into a billiard room.
— Villa di Careggi, just north of Florence, owned after 1848 by the Englishman Francis Sloane, who planted exotics in the garden, palms, cedars, and Californian sequoias; it is now a hospital.
— Villa di Castello (for which Botticelli's *Birth of Venus* was painted) is now the Accademia della Crusca and not open to the public.
— Villa di Cafaggiolo, available for conferences, wedding parties and corporate events.
— Villa di Pratolino, entry is free, to organize gala dinners contact the Soprintendenza.

Montisi, Tuscany, 1990
$3\frac{1}{2} \times 7^{31}/_{64}$" (9 × 19 CM)

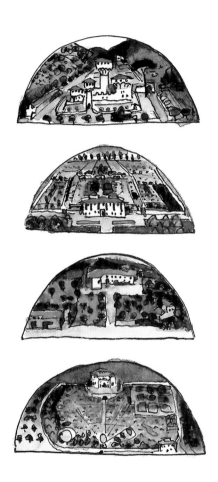

After Lunettes of the Medici villas by Giusto Utens, Florence, 1999
11 × 3½" (28 × 9 CM)

— Villa Collazzi, with a pool plonked in the middle of its cypress-lined lawn; since 2008 the home of Collazzi Libertà Toscana, a fine red wine.

— Villa le Barone, between Florence and Siena. Countess Franca Visconti transformed the sixteenth-century villa into an intimate hotel; today her descendants are happy to relate the villa's history to guests and direct them to the swimming pool, fitness room or tennis courts.

— Villa Corsini at Castello, now a museum, entry is free, weddings and other events possible.

— Villa le Maschere, a "Small Luxury Hotel," friendly and clean with a free shuttle service from the center of Florence.

— Villa Salviati, after passing through Italian, French, Swedish, and American hands, is now home to Historical Archives of the European Union.

— Villa Gamberaia, a hotel offering "perfect loveliness," as well as wedding planning courses. Garden visits cost 15 euros. Overlooking Florence, the villa boasts luxuriously appointed reception rooms, a nymphaeum and garden guest houses for holiday rental.

To be appropriated by Tafuri

King Kong dans le Boudoir, 1977
14 $^{61}/_{64}$ × 9 $^{27}/_{32}$" (38 × 25 CM)

Many were disappointed when *The Sphere and the Labyrinth*, the long-awaited English translation of Manfredo Tafuri's *La sfera e il labirinto*, finally appeared in 1987. Rather than the anticipated validation, it was a round denunciation of the current discourse of a self-fashioned avant-garde. Few apart from Rossi survived chapter 8, "L'architecture dans le boudoir," unscathed. The images of Archigram were "outmoded," Denys Lasdun and Leslie Martin were guilty of a "self-satisfied Englishness," while the New York Five sailed "closest to a conception of architecture as a means of reflecting upon itself." James Stirling's constructivist poetics did, however, win some praise, as an "interweaving of complex syntactic valences and ambiguous semantic references."

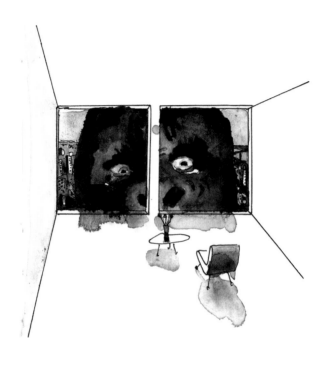

King Kong before Domestication, 2015

$3^{15}/_{16} \times 3^{15}/_{16}$” (10 × 10 CM)

Illustrations punctuating the weighty book begin with 11 Stirling images, a de Chirico painting and then nine images by Rossi interspersed with projects by Tessenow, Scolari, Aymonino, Purini, Gregotti, Venturi, Hollein, Isozaki, and Krier. Then, out of nowhere, illustration 314 is my own drawing of King Kong. How did it get there? Neither Tafuri nor the publisher had requested the image, but it didn't take long to deduce that the source was a 1978 issue of the Belgian magazine *AAM*, which had published it along with my rendering of *Une Maison Confortable (pour des Reveries Architecturales) dans la Grande Ville* on the facing page. Now in the Tafuri appropriation these two images shared the same page and were placed opposite Madelon Vriesendorp's *In Flagrante Delicto*, her iconic 1975 painting of the recumbent Empire State and Chrysler buildings that had graced the cover of Rem Koolhaas's 1978 *Delirious New York*.

Apart from the fact that copyright seemingly had no relevance in the stratosphere of Italian theory, the juxtaposition of King Kong with one of the most memorable images in Koolhaas's manifesto was entirely apt. As a teaching assistant in Koolhaas's and Elia Zenghelis's unit at the AA during *Delirious New York*'s gestation, I had been infected by a second-hand Manhattanism—a by-product of which was this careful rendering in deep chiaroscuro of a domesticated Kong, no longer climbing the exterior of the Empire State building but now comfortably enthroned on a giant porcelain WC in its cavernous interior. For Tafuri this infectious delirium evidenced an increasing withdrawal into the house of language, a playful plunge into the menagerie of a Barthean "pleasure of the text," which he cast as a parlour game dialectically opposed to the exhausted "ethical charge of twentieth-century avant-gardes." King Kong championed a recirculation of existing languages, a remythologizing thrust with the ambition to reinstate architecture's narrative dimension. This, for Tafuri, was a post-Babel fall into melancholic academicism.

To ask what happened to rationalism

By rationalism we refer to the ideal proportions that emerged in the mid-eighteenth century as a representation of Enlightenment reason—the geometric forms of Ledoux or Boullée, the functionalist principles of Carlo Lodoli, or the rigorous proto-scientific typologies of Jean-Nicolas-Louis Durand, for example.

Rationalism's reincarnation as *architettura razionale* instigated many reasons to travel to Italy between the 1920s and 1940s, among them the EUR and Adalberto Libera's post office in Rome, or Giuseppe Terragni's Casa del Fascio in Como. Gruppo 7's motto was "we do not intend to break with tradition ... the new architecture should be the result of a close association between logic and rationality." Next came *Tendenza*—an Italy-centered branch of neorationalism that emerged in the late 1960s through the work of Aldo Rossi, Giorgio Grassi, Carlo Aymonino, Franco Purini, and the writings of Manfredo Tafuri (1935–1994), then professor of architectural history at the University IUAV in Venice. Rossi's emphasis on typology and on monuments as expressions of collective memory resonated in Germany, where Josef Paul Kleihues, as director of the International Building Exhibition (IBA), was undertaking an eight-year "critical reconstruction of the European City." Oswald Mathias Ungers and disciples like Hans Kolhoff, Max Dudler, and Christoph Mäckler became the leading practitioners of German rationalism. Then, in 1980, the first-ever Venice Architecture Biennale would place this neorationalism in a wider context of American postmodernism, Japanese post-metabolism, and even poetic experiments from London.

Returning to Venice in 2013 to teach a workshop at the IUAV, we ask: what has happened to rationalism? The answer—a book—is pressed into our hands: the catalogue for the 2012 Nuova Architettura Razionale festival. But it does not offer any *ratio universalis*. Instead the introduction makes a rather desperate admission that "Rationalism is undergoing a profound crisis ... a pause is called for."

Written in both Italian and German, the catalogue reflects a certain collaborative partnership between two countries that still propagate rationalism. While the Italians theorize, the Germans construct buildings, as evidenced by rationalist-dominated post-unification construction in Berlin, or the reconstruction of the Berlin Schloss by German architects following the competition-winning design by former IUAV teacher Franco Stella. For Germans a reinvestigation of their 1930s architecture is not possible, whereas *architettura razionale* is continually undergoing reinterpretation. In the catalogue Armando dal Fabbro investigates a poetic transparency in the 1938 competition entries for the Palazzo dei Ricevimenti e dei Congressi by Libera and Terragni.

That the second generation has perhaps deviated from the stringencies of earlier rationalisms is demonstrated in a text by Jan Kleihues, who reasons that answering the question of "what is Architecture?" "requires an exact analysis of the architect's own expectations." Is this reflective subjectivity (and therefore contradictory to the dogmatic absolutism we associate with rationalism)? Propping up his statement is the assertion that "context is the origin of all architecture" (the site-specific overrides the universal nature of typologies). Finally, for good measure, "atmosphere" (that catchphrase of phenomenology) is thrown in as an attribute of rationalism. It is not difficult to conclude that in the business of construction the repetitive window is less an ideological signpost and more a financial expedient.

To collect snails and slaves

Lady Arundel returned to England in 1662 with a collection of paintings, a gondola, two black slaves, a consignment of edible snails, and a model of Giulio Romano's Palazzo del Te, a building which Inigo Jones, her *cicerone* some ten years earlier, had admired.

To verify the magnetism of a name

Almost seven percent of the population of Perugia is made up of foreign citizens. Among this minority, the third largest group comes from Peru (Peruvians in Perugia are outnumbered only by Albanians and Moroccans).

To be reviled by a "revived paganism"

In the 1830s A. W. N. Pugin (1812–1852)—future creator of the gothic revival Palace of Westminster—denounced the "foolish education of many architectural students who, after idling a few years on the classical soils of Greece or Italy and having measured for the hundredth time the remains of some fractured column or restored a whole amphitheater from a few feet of stone seat, return to their countries and venture to attempt styles." He himself had a much more solid basis for his career, beginning his medieval fundamentalist campaign dressed in a sailor's costume, importing chunks of Flemish gothic buildings that had been discarded across the Channel.

Pugin, a Catholic convert, contrasted the gothic—"the glorious works produced by faith, zeal and devotion of the middle ages"—with the "revived classical," which he equated with a "revived paganism," impious, sensual, egotistical. On his one, reluctant, visit to Italy in 1847 he was surprised to find many fine examples of gothic architecture; fortunately, a visit to the Vatican allowed him to revert to script and pronounce "the Sistine Chapel ... a melancholy room, the *Last Judgement* ... a painfully muscular delineation of a glorious subject, the Scala Regia a humbug, the Vatican a hideous mass, and St Peter's ... the greatest failure of all."

To speak the lingo

After Bruno Munari, *Supplement to the Italian Dictionary*, 2015
All 3⁵⁄₃₂ × 3⁵⁄₃₂" (8 × 8 CM)

To avoid being insane in America

Ezra Pound, 2022
$3^{15}/_{16} \times 3^{15}/_{16}$" (10 × 10 CM)

T. S. Eliot dedicated *The Waste Land* to his fellow poet, the American Ezra Pound (1885–1972), whom he called "*il miglior fabbro*" (the better craftsman). This was the same phrase Dante Aligheri had used to praise his twelfth-century precursor, Arnaut Daniel. Pound, enmeshed in the milieu of early modernism, had selflessly promoted Eliot and helped edit his work. He also provided James Joyce with the financial support that enabled him to complete *Ulysses*.

As a child Pound made a number of tours to Italy with his family and undertook his first solo journey at the age of 23. When he was 36, he abandoned England, imagism and vorticism to live in Paris (1921–24). There he fell in with Marcel Duchamp, Tristan Tzara, and the rest of the dada and surrealist troupe. In 1923 he toured Italy with Hemingway, and a year later he moved to Rome. Reacting to the carnage of the First World War and what he termed the usury of the British, he took up the cause of Mussolini's fascism. For his wartime radio broadcasts issued from Rome, Pound was declared a traitor in

America. In 1945, advancing American troops caught up with him in Pisa, where they held him for three weeks like a zoo animal in an outdoor cage (instigating a mental breakdown). On the eve of his trial for treason he was declared insane and forced to spend 12 years in American mental hospitals. During this time he penned *Pisan Cantos*, which won the 1948 Bollingen Library of Congress Award for the best book of verse by an American author. The recognition drew criticism from Robert Hillyer, a professor of literature at Harvard University, who saw in the award "evidence of a complex conspiracy against American ways of life." A joint committee later determined that no further Congressional cultural prizes would be given. Thanks to a campaign undertaken by his fellow writers ("Great poets are not necessarily girl guides nor scoutmasters nor splendid influences on youth," Hemingway told the *Paris Review*), Pound was declared incurably insane but "harmless enough" to be released from hospital in 1958. On hearing this news, Pound—by now an ashen old man of 72 years—announced to journalists as he boarded a ship for Italy, "Any man who could live in America is insane."

In *The Skin* (1949), Curzio Malaparte describes Pound, along with T. S. Eliot and Isadora Duncan, as "iridescent flies caught in the black web of an ancient and amoral European culture."

To be captured by the Ospedale degli Innocenti

Ostensibly my reason for being in Florence was to give a lecture to a group of American students. The location was Filippo Brunelleschi's Ospedale degli Innocenti (Foundling Hospital) facing the Piazza Santissima Annunziata. Afterwards Adolfo Natalini proudly told us that it had been his initiative, some 30 years earlier, that had banished cars from the square.

Approaching the hospital diagonally from the hotel— a maneuver made possible by the car-vanishing act performed by the ex-Superstudioist—I was captured by the way that Brunelleschi's architrave, on hitting the left and right extremities of the arched facade, abruptly turns a right angle and heads towards the ground. This, according to the German art historian Wolfgang Kemp, is a big mistake, and one that can be attributed to the fact that Brunelleschi did not supervise the building site, or so he informs us, citing Giorgio Vasari's explanation. When left to their own devices, the masons apparently reverted to the medieval tradition of plaque-framing architraves—a cause of some anguish to Kemp, who insists that architraves should never be given the function of a column since they are in essence and origin horizontal, a gathering and transferring of the weight of the wall above. As one might expect in a German context, Kemp's analytical method is based on a rigorous designation of correct and incorrect, a canonical absolutism that can have no truck with errorism, whether willful or the outcome of neglect.

A more sympathetic reading of the naughty Brunelleschi architrave might construe that added to the force of gravity pressing down on the hospital facade there is also a force from the sides—the weight of the surroundings, of the context, of medievalism, of an entirely Romanesque fifteenth-century Florence through which Brunelleschi's classical facade cut a window onto the Renaissance.

Brunelleschi's Naughty Architrave + Scarpa Toys With Brunelleschi's Mistake—Entrance to Philosophy Faculty, Venice, 2021
$3\frac{1}{2} \times 7\frac{3}{32}$" (9 × 18 CM)

To survey the coast

In 1550 a 20-year-old Thomas Hoby, one of the first Englishmen to tour southern Italy, set out by boat from Civitavecchia for Naples. Having rounded Monte Circello (associated, in mythology, with the enchantress Circe) he wrote, in apparent trepidation, "we sayled all the night … in a little port, under the hill lye manie times Moores and Turks in their foistes and other vesselles to take the passinger vesselles that goo betwixt Roome and Naples … yf we had cum by daye … we had bine all taken slaves."

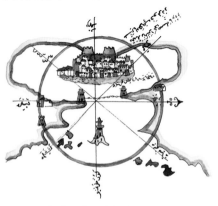

Brindisi after Piri Reis, 2013
$3^{15}/_{16} \times 3^{15}/_{16}$" (10 × 10 CM)

The Moorish marauders that Hoby took pains to avoid were possibly ex-crew members of the Ottoman commander/pirate Piri Reis, who was at that moment plying his trade in the Arabian Sea, having crossed overland from Egypt (with dismantled ships) and taken Aden in February 1549. In 1552, armed with 25 vessels and 850 Suez soldiers, he set out to harass the Portuguese East India fleet. His reputation as a mapmaker had been assured in 1513, when he presented his first world map to Suleyman the Magnificent. As well as precise surveys of

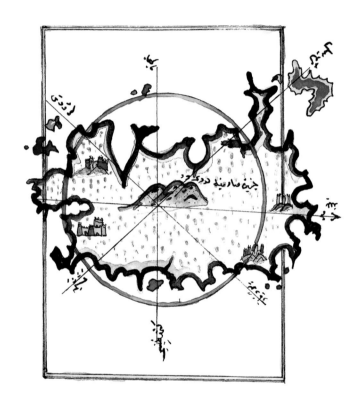

Sardinia after Piri Reis, 2013
$3\,^{15}\!/_{16} \times 3\,^{15}\!/_{16}$" (10 × 10 CM)

Italy's shores (of interest to all diligent pirates), this included the latest topographical information for the coasts of India, the Atlantic, and even South America (most likely gleaned from members of Columbus' crew). The map visualizes fortifications, cities, and harbors while reducing the coastline to strings of scimitar-like bays, an emblematic visual trope that overlays not only strategic value but also a specific syntactic calligraphy—a form of visualization evidencing a parallel Ottoman cultural and aesthetic regime. Unlike the utility of pirates' charts, here a land-bound gaze interrogates the horizon and the latent defensive and picturesque qualities of coastal topography.

To see a beach

Visits to the beach were not on the itinerary for grand tourists, unlike contemporary travelers to Italy. When did beach-blindness begin to abate? With the mapping of coastlines? With a nineteenth-century interest in physical culture (subsequently instrumentalized by fascism)? Or when the majority of visitors to Italy had learned to swim and the science of sun creams was advanced enough to offer protection to pale northern skin? The Italian beach started to become a recognizable theme through the works of painters like Jakob Philipp Hackert, who, after sojourns painting harbors and coasts for the Swedish king, as well as experience of Flemish and French (Normandy) landscape painting, arrived in Rome in 1769. The following year, while painting for Sir William Hamilton in Naples, he retreated to Vietri sul Mare to recover from a fever. While convalescing he sketched the cliffs, grottos and water reflections of the Amalfi coast. Oscar Wilde once said that there was no fog in London before Whistler painted it. Equally, there were no beaches in Italy until Hackert painted them. The coast had to be painted before it could be seen. The new visual paradigm of the Romantic coastline was further disseminated into the European cultural consciousness by the panoramas painted by the Italian watercolorist Giovanni Battista

Lusieri (Hackert's rival) and, later, the Neapolitan Saverio della Gatta. Hackert's coastal documentation and production of seductive images of beaches and harbors became official with a commissioned series documenting the ports and harbors belonging to Ferdinand of Naples. These aestheticized an often ruinous actuality with bright colors (for the king's Sicilian taste), much like blue photoshopped beaches seen today when one googles "beach-Italy."

By the late eighteenth century, as Hackert was manufacturing his coastal imagery, sea bathing was coming into fashion in England— its medicinal benefits having long been propagated by Dr Richard Russell. With the parading of the Prince of Wales's exquisite circle, the fishing village of Brightelmstone (Brighton) became both a center of fashion and the prototypical beach resort. Dieppe in France and Heiligendamm in Germany were also places for society to enter the ocean. English dilettanti would only have to look at the Hackerts on their walls to be struck by the idea of transposing the concept of sea immersion to the more agreeable climate of Italy.

After Jakob Philipp Hackert, *Marina Piccola in Sorrento*, 2013
$3^{15}/_{16} \times 4^{21}/_{64}$" (10 × 11 CM)

Some Pools and Beaches, Including Amalfi + Capri, 2014
$5\frac{3}{32} \times 1\frac{37}{64}$" (13 × 4 CM)

To build a Palladian Capanna

In Venice, guests at the Grand Hotel Excelsior can hire a *capanna* or beach hut (a minimal cube of architecture—Rossi's reading) fronting the Adriatic for €14,000 per season. Prices fall to €4,500 for the second and third rows.

In 1998 Bolles+Wilson were commissioned to install a temporary pavilion (24 hours) inside the refectory of San Giorgio Maggiore. The project—Palladio's Capanna—was designed as module components small enough to be transported by boat across the lagoon and then assembled in the grand refectory—essentially relocating the Lido beach hut inside the church. In its virtual afterlife Palladio's Capanna migrated back to the warm twilight glow of the Lido beach.

Palladio's Capanna I, 2013
$4^{11}/_{16} \times 4^{11}/_{16}$" (12 × 12 CM)

Palladio's Capanna II, 2013
4 $^{11}/_{16}$ × 4 $^{11}/_{16}$" (12 × 12 CM)

Palladio's Capanna goes Lido, 2013
7 $^{3}/_{32}$ × 9 $^{13}/_{16}$" (18 × 25 CM)

To peruse a futurist coastline

When Luigi Russolo and Filippo Tommaso Marinetti gave the first concert of futurist music in 1914, a riot broke out. Their Gran Concerto Futuristico of 1917 was also met with violence. But to the contemporary urban dweller, motorist or, for that matter, holidaymaker, Russolo's sound taxonomy would not be cause for alarm. Roars, thundering, bangs and booms, shouts, screams, hoots, whispers, murmurs, and mutterings, as well as noises obtained by beating on metal, wood, and pottery, and rustling, buzzing, crackling, and scraping all have their place in his compositions, as detailed in his *Art of Noises* (1913). His networks of sound collages favored dissonance, as opposed to the synthesizing unity and symmetrical qualities of other projects such as the *Città Nuova* or design for a power station of fellow futurist Antonio Sant'Elia.

Towards the end of the twentieth century Russolo's compositional hypothesis materialized in linear form as a futurist coastline, booming through mountain-penetrating tunnels and whizzing over valley-spanning bridges stretched parallel to the Ligurian coast. Not quite as materially imposing as Le Corbusier's proposals for Algiers or Rio de Janeiro (inspired by his 1934 drive on the roof of the Turin Fiat Factory) or Luigi Carlo Danieri's "Il Biscione" (1956–58), a snaking wall of 850 apartments hugging the cliffs near Genoa, today's futurist coastline exhibits a heterogeneous formatting, a collage of scales, organizational protocols, representational currencies and temporal markers. Some of these are familiar manifestations of pan-European transportational modalities and distribution systems.

One can imagine the eulogies of circulation that underpin the glinting carpets of stepped glass houses that face south on Ligurian hills for the most efficient ripening of tomatoes (seeded in the Netherlands), destined to travel further south (where packaging and labeling pick up a healthy EU subsidy) to become vacuum-packed pizzas sold in German supermarkets.

Ligurian Coast, 2002

3 15/16 × 3 15/16" (10 × 10 CM)

Futurist Coastline, 2002

$2\frac{3}{4} \times 8\frac{17}{64}$" (7 × 21 CM)

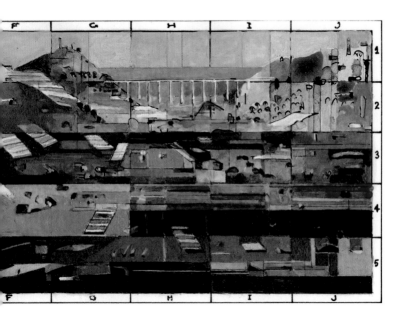

Train tracks, the first futurist invasion of this rustic Mediterranean perimeter, follow and tag the coast, with beaches accessed only through their viaduct arches—it was these very structures that first brought the prosperity of summer invaders. Tracks pass behind towns and fishing villages now swamped with the tic-tac of postcards and beach equipment. Most Italian summer invaders stay in *pensioni*, while further up fertile valleys entire villages are in German hands. Here, in front of baroque village churches, mayors organize summer concerts starring Japanese opera singers (probably studying in Milan). Beachside campsites are packed with Dutch caravans (the Dutch have no fear of high water). Floating precipitously above the intertwining layers of coastal exploitation are the leaf-bound pixels of the Italian villa strata. Out at sea white luxury yachts disentangle themselves from the futurist soup, and even further out one imagines the distressed and desparate craft of illegal immigrants, risking their lives to join the mix.

It seems from this example that it is not necessary today for the physicality, the obdurate materiality of architecture, to prefigure futurist scenarios. These now play out in spatio-temporal geographies, overlaid protocols and elastic boundary conditions. The ecologies of circuitry, and in particular the art of visual noise, characterize this choreography of distribution systems and its corollary landscape of dispersed and overlapping spatial tropes. Such ephemeral logistics tend to become visible only when negotiating complex and mountainous topographies, as is the case along the Ligurian coast. But still we nostalgically like to imagine that the voluminous mirage extending from the next cape toward the azure Mediterranean horizon might in fact be an architecture worthy of the name futurist.

To Google Earth it

Headquarters of Google Earth it, 2013
6 ¹⁹⁄₆₄ × 11" (16 × 28 CM)

Today it is of course possible to survey the seductive contours of the Italian landscape without ever experiencing them firsthand. But the charms of Google Earth are somewhat wanting in terms of substance and material: no siennas, no umbers, no earth even. Speculation along these lines leads to an imagined institutional manifestation of Google's appropriations of the surface of the earth—a specifically Italian Google Earth Headquarters, planted right in the terrain it maps, as a collision of both scales. But an edifice such as this, set against a rolling landscape, must pump iron in order to assert its presence—an inhabited billboard of absolute architecture weaving its serpentine tail into field folds, the striations of agriculture, traditional farmhouses, production sheds and grape-facilitating grids.

To collaborate

In 1985 the Italian architect Bruno Minardi was invited to participate in an exhibition proposing new buildings for Rome, but he thought the city already had enough good architecture. Instead, he designed a roving building—a machine that would move about the city, cleaning and maintaining noble edifices. This was a big task. Therefore mindful Minardi invited me to collaborate on the design for an assistant machine, a sidekick with extendable boom arm for reaching difficult corners. By day, the two maintainers, although related, would pursue independent trajectories. At night, for comfort, security, or mutual maintenance, they would clip together in a matrimonial embrace.

Roving Maintainer + Sidekick Embrace, 1985
$2\,^{23}\!/_{64} \times 2\,^{23}\!/_{64}$" (6 × 6 CM)

Carlo Scarpa, Museo Canova, Possagno, 2004
3¹⁵⁄₁₆ × 5½" (10 × 14 CM)

264

ACKNOWLEDGEMENTS

The idea for a book of reasons to travel south first took root in 2011 when the Italian publishers Moleskine approached Bolles+Wilson to assemble a notebook already full of sketches, one of the first of their "Inspiration and Process in Architecture" series—a commission that brought into focus the fact that trips in relation to our Italian projects were in a way reenactments of longstanding Grand Tour templates. It was Thomas Weaver, then editor of *AA Files* at the Architectural Association, who suggested publishing a handful of these reasons in his journal, and who subsequently expanded the initial clutch of anecdotes into a dedicated book and exhibition. This was with his excellent and now tragically disbanded AA team of Pamela Johnston, Sarah Handelman, and Claire Lyon. The current enlarged and revised version is also due to the vision of Thomas, now in his navigating role at the MIT Press. For his support, gentle nudges, and not-to-be underestimated input I am greatly indebted. Our ensuing conversations have been wonderfully uplifting in dark pandemic times. I would also like to thank Rosa Nussbaum for her elegant and compelling graphic layout of this MIT Press edition and Matthew Abbate for his expert copy-editing.

Along the way, critical advice from Eva Wilson and Gerd Blum has helped with embellishments and corrections, and Kurt W. Foster's more than generous introductory words have further added a veil of academicism. A big *danke* to Julia Bolles-Wilson for putting up with this madness for so long, and to my team at Bolles+Wilson (Stephanie Eikelman, Heike Breiden, Mura Mroz, and Kristina Schröder) for endless scans. There are also many visible and invisible mentors and colleagues who have provided unflagging encouragement, among them Carlos Ascenco, who engineered a Spanish version of the Hackert text, and Francisco Sanin, who often provided me with reasons to travel to Italy, guiding me past Brunelleschi and on to the Traffic Island of the Dead.

BIBLIOGRAPHY

Mary Bergstein, *Mirrors of Memory: Freud, Photography and the History of Art* (Ithaca, NY: Cornell University Press, 2010)

Jeremy Black, *Italy and the Grand Tour* (New Haven, CT: Yale University Press, 2003)

Carol Blackett-Ord, "Letters from William Kent to Burrell Massingberd from the Continent, 1712–1719," *The Volume of the Walpole Society* 63 (2001), 75–109.

Gordon Burn, "Writing on the Wall," *The Guardian*, June 14, 2008

Robert Burton, *The Anatomy of Melancholy* (London: J. M. Dent, 1932)

Edward Chaney, *The Evolution of the Grand Tour* (London: Routledge, 1988)

Edward Chaney, *The Grand Tour and the Great Rebellion: Richard Lassels and "The Voyage of Italy" in the Seventeenth Century* (Geneva: Slatkine, 1985)

Steven Connor, *The Matter of Air: Science and the Art of the Ethereal* (London: Reaktion Books, 2010)

Caroline Constant, *The Woodland Cemetery: Toward a Spiritual Landscape, Erik Gunnar Asplund and Sigurd Lewerentz, 1915–61* (Stockholm: Byggförlaget, 1994)

J. Mordaunt Crook, *The Greek Revival: Neo-Classical Attitudes in British Architecture 1760–1870* (London: John Murray, 1972)

Nicholas Cullinan, et al, *Twombly and Poussin, Arcadian Painters* (London: Dulwich Picture Gallery in association with Paul Holbertson, 2011)

Nicholas Cullinan, Nicholas Serota, et al, *Cy Twombly: Cycles and Seasons* (New York: Distributed Art Publishers, 2008)

Cy Twombly, Paintings and Drawings, 1954–1977, exhibition catalogue (New York: Whitney Museum of American Art, 1979)

Pierre Alexandre de Loosz, "Cy Twombly 1966," *032c* 19 (2010)

Richard Dorment, "The Dilettanti: Exclusive Society that Celebrates Art," *Daily Telegraph*, September 2, 2008

The Earl of March, *A Duke and His Friends: The Life and Letters of the Second Duke of Richmond* (London: Hutchinson & Co, 1911)

Paulo Farina, "Puzzle-City: Milan, Transfigurations at the Fragment," *Daidalos* 16 (1985), 81–91

John Fleming, *Robert Adam and His Circle* (Cambridge, MA: Harvard University Press, 1962)

Nicola Flora, et al, *Sigurd Lewerentz, 1885–1975* (Milan: Electa Architecture, 2002)

Antonio Foscari, *Tumult and Order: Malcontenta, 1924–1939* (Zurich: Lars Müller Publishers, 2012)

Jakob Philipp Hackert: Europas Landschaftsmaler der Goethezeit (Stuttgart: Hatje Kantz, 2008)

John Harris, "With William Kent at Burlington House," Royal Academy, 2014

Rosemary Hill, *God's Architect: Pugin and the Building of Romantic Britain* (New Haven, CT: Yale University Press, 2007)

Hans Holenweg, "Die Toteninsel: Arnold Böcklin's populäres Landschaftsbild und seine Ausstrahlung bis in die heutige Zeit," *Das Münster* 54 (2001), 235–41

Elizabeth Vassall Fox Holland, *The Journal of Elizabeth Lady Holland* (London: Longmans Green, and Co, 1908)

John Ingamells, *A Dictionary of British and Irish Travellers in Italy, 1701 –1800, Compiled from the Brinsley Ford Archive* (London: Paul Mellon Centre for Studies in British Art, 1997)

Gabriele Katz, *Angelika Kauffmann: Künstlerin and Geschäftsfrau* (Stuttgart: Belser, 2012)

Angelica Kauffmann, *Angelica Kauffmann, RA: Her Life and Her Works* (London: Lane, 1924)

August Kestner and Charlotte Kestner, *Briefwechsel zwischen August Kestner und seiner Schwester Charlotte* (Strasbourg: Karl F. Trubner, 1904)

Mario Tedeschini Lalli, "Descent from Paradise: Saul Steinberg's Italian Years (1933–1941)," *Quest: Issues in Contemporary Jewish History, Journal of Fondazione CDEC*, October 2, 2011

Grace Lees-Maffei, *Writing Design: Words and Objects* (London: Berg, 2012)

"'A Little Bit of Magic Realised': William Henry Fox Talbot and his Circle," *The Metropolitan Museum of Art Bulletin* 56/4 (1999), 4–11

Cecile Lowenthal-Hensel and Jutta Arnold, *Wilhelm Hensel, Maler und Portraitist, 1794–1861* (Berlin: Mann, 2004)

Curzio Malaparte, *The Skin* (New York: New York Review of Books Classics, 2013)

Lady Anna Riggs Miller, *Letters from Italy: Describing the Manners, Customs, Antiquities, Paintings, etc of That Country* (London: Edward and Charles Dilly, 1777)

L. B. Namier, John Brooke, *The History of Parliament: the House of Commons 1754–1790* (New York: Oxford University Press, 1964)

Mine Esiner Ozen, *Piri Reis and His Charts* (Istanbul: N. Refioglu Publications, 1998)

Sabine Rewald, *Rooms with a View: The Open Window in the Nineteenth Century* (New Haven, CT: Yale University Press, 2001)

Gottfried Semper, *Preliminary Remarks on Polychrome Architecture and Sculpture in Antiquity* (New York: Cambridge University Press, 1989)

Dmitriĭ Shvidkovskii, *The Empress & the Architect: British Architecture and Gardens at the Court of Catherine the Great* (New Haven, CT: Yale University Press, 1996)

Patricia Meyer Spacks, "Splendid Falsehoods: English Accounts of Rome, 1760–1798," *Prose Studies* 3/3 (1980), 203–16

Laurence Sterne, *A Sentimental Journey* (London: Penguin Classics, 2001)

Martino Stierli, "In the Academy's Garden: Robert Venturi, the Grand Tour and the Revision of Modernism," *AA Files* 56 (2007), 42–63

Martino Stierli, *Venturi's Grand Tour: On the Genealogy of Postmodernism* (Basel: Standpunkte, 2011)

Mariana Starke, *Travels in Italy Between the Years 1792 and 1798* (London: R. Phillips, 1802)

Heidi Strobel, "Reviewed Works: Miss Angel: The Art and World of Angelica Kauffmann by Angelica Goodden; Angelica Kauffmann: Art and Sensibility by Angela Rosenthal," *Woman's Art Journal* 29/1 (2008), 45–48

Dorothy Stroud, *Sir John Soane Architect* (London: Faber and Faber, 1984)

David Sylvester, *Interviews with American Artists* (New Haven, CT: Yale University Press, 2001)

Léa-Catherine Szacka, "The 1980 Architecture Biennale: The Street as a Spatial and Representational Curating Device," *OASE 88: Exhibitions* (2012), 14–25

Alina Szapocznikow, "Patinoire dans le cratère du Vésuve," typescript illustration 7380, Alina Szapocznikow Archive

Manfredo Tafuri, *The Sphere and the Labyrinth: Avant-Gardes and Architecture from Piranesi to the 1970s* (Cambridge, MA: MIT Press, 1987)

Robert Venturi, *Iconography and Electronics upon a Generic Architecture* (Cambridge, MA: MIT Press, 1996), 42

Horace Walpole, *The Letters of Horace Walpole, Fourth Earl of Orford* (London: University of Oxford, 1903)

Aidan Weston-Lewis, et al, *Expanding Horizons: Giovanni Battista Lusieri and the Panoramic Landscape* (Edinburgh: National Gallery of Scotland, 2012)

Giles Worsley, "Master Builder: Lord Burlington," *Daily Telegraph*, April 5, 2003

Roberto Zapperi, *All Roads Lead to Rome: The Eternal City and Its Visitors* (Berlin: C. H. Beck, 2013)

Cino Zucchi, *Innesti/Grafting, The Venice Biennale 14th International Architecture Exhibition*, vol 2 (Venice: Marsilio, 2014)

To note and record

Long before the English made a fashion of touring the Italian peninsula, the Romans paid them a visit. Julius Agricola, governor of London from 77 to 84 AD, reported on progress made in assisting the bellicose "Britons to build temples, fora and homes" and "to be less warlike, to learn Latin, rhetoric, to become accustomed to the pleasures of leisure"—a seduction into a newfound set of alluring vices, Agricola continued, that "the simple natives called *humanitas*, when it was really a facet of their enslavement." Continuing this unequal traffic some two millennia later, the fragmented, perhaps still fundamentally simple, experiences recorded here attempt to add an unexpected and often contradictory dimension to both the now over-familiar genre of the Grand Tour and the even more familiar genre of Italy as a whole. For an architect, no matter how much one reasons on these mythologies from the distance of a northern European living room and the abstraction of a book, a real encounter with a country and with the very physicality of its buildings—their presence, materials, and smells, as well as the fact that they are anchored to one particular location—is always a special and arresting moment. And while taking architectural notes is a distraction from this phenomenological engagement, it is equally a means of analyzing, of slowing down, of filtering and digesting these encounters with architecture. To draw a building or a place is a little act of homage; it is also a small theft—one selects and appropriates, carries off an imprint; one's own take. Luckily, buildings are as generous as they are robust; they are not depleted but fortified by such encounters. As for the drawings themselves, they subsequently fall into that vast traffic of ideas and images we call culture. And are all the better for this descent.

How Grand My Tour, after Giovanni Paolo Panini, 2010
$4\,^{59}\!/_{64} \times 4\,^{59}\!/_{64}$" ($12.5 \times 12.5$ CM)

Some Reasons for Traveling to Italy
Peter Wilson

© 2022 Massachusetts Institute of Technology

Originally published in 2016 as
Some Reasons for Travelling to Italy
by the Architectural Association, London

Edited by Thomas Weaver
Designed by Studio Christopher Victor
This book was set in Heldane Text and Salter
Printed and bound in Italy by Musumeci

Library of Congress Cataloging-in-Publication Data is available.

ISBN: 978-0-262-04726-5

10 9 8 7 6 5 4 3 2 1

Above Ulysses, the first to travel to Italy, 2016
Frontispiece Dr James Hays, Bear-leader, after Pier Leone Ghezzi, 2014